I had the privilege to work on the same pastoral staff with Jill Maria Murdy as she developed her strategy and resources for enhancing funeral ministry in the parish. Her approach balances good theology and practical advice. At a time when a growing number of contemporary funeral directors almost seem to be "marketing" services to grieving families by promoting secular memorials, Jill Maria provides a helpful path for retaining the power of the Catholic ritual to address the reality of death and bring healing and hope through the celebration of the promise of the resurrection.

Most Reverend Jeffrey R. Haines, *Auxiliary Bishop, Archdiocese of Milwaukee*

In this insightful pastoral resource, Jill Maria covers many of the issues and societal changes that have emerged since the *Order of Christian Funerals* was promulgated almost thirty years ago. Filled with practical advice and thoughtful theological reflection, this book should be on the shelf of every priest, musician, and pastoral minister who deals with funerals.

Christopher Ferraro, *Director of Music, Our Lady of Perpetual Help Church, Lindenhurst, NY*

Jill Maria Murdy has written a wonderful, pastoral, practical, personal, liturgical, and theological resource for anyone involved in ministry to persons preparing for the celebration of the funeral of a loved one, or preparing for their own funeral. I am adding it to the required texts for a class that I teach on the *Order of Christian Funerals*. It will help our society view death as part of life, and grief as part of the journey into eternal life.

Rev. Paul H. Colloton, OSFS, D.Min., *Priest Chaplain and Director of Campus Ministry, Ohio Dominican University*

Changing times, changing mores. Death and dying in the American context have evolved over the decades and continue to do so. Just to mention a few developments, hospice is involved more and more in the events surrounding death, and many more people are choosing cremation as the preferred way to deal with the mortal remains of loved ones. These present challenges for the *Order of Christian Funerals* published in 1985 and revised in 1989. Jill Maria offers concrete, practical, and pastoral measures on how the Order can be applied in these changing times.

Michael S. Driscoll, *Professor Emeritus, University of Notre Dame*

A Parish Guide for BEREAVEMENT MINISTRY & FUNERAL PLANNING

JILL MARIA MURDY

TWENTY-THIRD PUBLICATIONS
twentythirdpublications.com

For my family,
and in memory of my mother, Rosemarie;

for the Sisters of Sacred Heart Monastery,

for Saint Frances Cabrini Parish,

You have all taught me so much about life and death,
And I am ever grateful.

JILL MARIA

TWENTY-THIRD PUBLICATIONS
One Montauk Avenue, Suite 200
New London, CT 06320
(860) 437-3012 or (800) 321-0411
www.twentythirdpublications.com

ISBN: 978-1-62785-392-7
Library of Congress Control Number: 2018943421
Printed in the U.S.A.

A division of Bayard, Inc.

CONTENTS

PROLOGUE

O death! How bitter is the thought of you
  for the one at peace in his home,
For the one who is serene and always successful,
  who can still enjoy life's pleasures.
O death! How welcome is your sentence to the weak,
  failing in strength,
Stumbling and tripping on everything,
  with sight gone and hope lost.
Do not fear death's decree for you;
Remember, it embraces those before you and those to come.

■ **Sirach (Ecclesiasticus) 41:1–3**

If we spend any time in parish funeral ministry, we will surely experience both these extremes. There are tragic deaths of children, those who die suddenly in car accidents and in violent situations, the death of police officers and soldiers, or young adults dying from a terminal illness. Similarly, there are times when an elderly person has been dying for so long that death is indeed welcome, when the pain of an illness has been so extreme the family is just glad that the struggle is over.

When a parish gets a call about an incoming funeral, it puts many different wheels in motion. Likely, an administrative assistant will be the first one to take a call on a funeral, and will be making calls and sending texts or emails trying to coordinate with priests, ministers, and funeral home, while also juggling the facilities calendar to schedule a time to meet with family members for planning, and times for the Vigil service, funeral, luncheon, and Rite of Committal.

Often, when we meet with a family, we do not know what the story is until they arrive. We know that it will be emotional and that we must be prepared to help the family through any situation. In my own life, I have sat on both sides of that planning table, and it is never easy; but is so very important to do it reverently and well! In this book, I include information about the rites in general, along with particular examples based upon my understanding of death. This book, then, is a mixture of knowledge acquired along the way in my profession, my own personal experiences, and research in areas that were foreign to me. It is my prayer that this book will provide you with tools to help those you serve sing the resurrection song!

Jill Maria Murdy, July 2018

CHAPTER ONE

The World We Live In

Once upon a time, it might have been safe to assume that a family coming in to plan a funeral would all be Catholic, and that ninety percent of those attending the funeral would likely be Catholic too. Most would likely be from the parish. In many cases, the family really didn't have any input into the Scripture readings, and the same basic hymnody might be employed for most funerals. Those with memories of pre-Vatican II liturgies may recall the haunting Latin *Dies Irae* and the *In Paradisum* ending the liturgy.

Though there have been no changes to the *Order of Christian Funerals* since 1985/89, society has been through many transitions. The way we grieve is different. Many cultural traditions, including wakes that lasted several days, no longer happen. In many ways we have sanitized death and tried to make it as quick and pain free as possible. As Richard P. Taylor tells us in his book, *Death and the Afterlife*,

> the wake is observed today only by some Roman Catholics and by Orthodox Jews. At the beginning of the twenty-first century, it is much more common for the deceased to be removed from the home very quickly (if he or she is not already away from home, dying in a hospital or hospice). The local coroner or attending physician is called to complete an official certificate of death, and the body is soon transported to a morgue or funeral home. Thus, religious traditions play little part of the funerary customs of Christians today until the body has been handled by secular professionals, cosmetically altered, placed in a coffin, and made ready for transport to the funeral service.
> ▪ ***Death and the Afterlife*, Funerary Customs, p. 129**

This is echoed in an essay by Charles O. Jackson entitled "Death Shall Have No Dominion" in *Death and Dying: Views from Many Cultures*. There he tells us:

> the dead world has been largely lost because an increasingly temporal and secular-minded living world has actively chosen to abandon even the topic itself. Though hardly news, it should be noted here nonetheless that in this century death has become a taboo. Very little relationship is possible with a realm which we are rigorously seeking to forget....In a culture which will support no longer the certainty of afterlife, natural death and physical decomposition have become too horrible to contemplate or discuss. ▪ ***Death and Dying*, p. 52**

Much has changed in recent years. Families have spread out, and many times the children of the deceased are nonpracticing Catholics or they have moved on to another tradition, likely a nondenominational church that is almost the polar opposite of the Catholic ritual. In the Catholic rite itself, the post-Vatican II ritual has more emphasis on hope in the resurrection. However, many times the liturgy gets stuck in an almost cookie-cutter format with "Amazing Grace," "How Great Thou Art," "Here I Am, Lord," "Be Not Afraid," "On Eagle's Wings," and "Shepherd Me, O God." (*Note:* Nothing is wrong with these songs; they just don't have to be the automatic choices. This will be discussed in a later chapter.)

Occasionally, family members trying to get a jump on planning go to the internet and YouTube, where they may come up with ideas like Vince Gill's "Go Rest High Upon a Mountain," or Frank Sinatra's "My Way." They come in with prayer poems with titles like "It was God's Plan" that may be comforting to them but have no place in the liturgy. They mean no harm and are thinking of their loved ones, so it is necessary in these situations to deal with them in as kind and pastoral a way as possible, while still respecting the rites. It means that clear and honest explanations of the ritual and a discerning heart are necessary in working with them. What we do not need to do at this time is reinvent the liturgy. Rather we need to follow the rites as best we can and let their inherent richness help the family involved celebrate the Rite of Christian Burial.

It is safe to say that most people do not have a clear understanding of the *Order of Christian Funerals*, and that for various reasons, neither parishes or funeral homes often encourage the Rite in its full form today. A lot of factors influence this: people's understanding of the rites themselves, mobile family traveling in from all over, the working society of today, the schedules of churches and funeral homes, and the almighty dollar itself.

Many years ago, early in this author's parish ministry, there was a case where a woman died. She was a daily Massgoer, and her faith was part and parcel of her very being. Sadly, her kids did not go to church, so they said, "Just do a little service at the funeral home." Both the priest and I angsted over this woman not receiving a full Mass of Christian Burial, so we began talking about how we could help other folks in that situation. It was at that time that we decided we wanted to help people prepare in advance, so that they might understand the rites and their wishes might be respected. We began to offer funeral planning workshops in our parish. In the next chapter we will talk about those workshops and preplanning in general.

CHAPTER TWO

Preplanning for Funerals

One of the easiest mistakes to make as a professional minister or a trained volunteer is to presume knowledge. In our fields, we work with death and funeral rituals so much they can become commonplace and just another thing on our calendar for a busy day or week. But for those looking at death for the first time, there are a lot of unknowns out there. It is not uncommon for funeral homes to sell prepackaged deals, but that usually amounts to getting a plot and getting details lined up and paid for, and doesn't usually include any of the fine points dealing with the funeral rite itself. So let us take a look at how we can address some of those questions.

The parish I serve offers a funeral planning workshop once or twice a year, and we also schedule individual planning meetings as requested to better assist people. Below are topics addressed in our planning sessions that might be helpful to you. We start before death itself, by explaining the difference between anointing of the sick and last rites.

ANOINTING OF THE SICK, LAST RITES, AND PRAYERS FOR THE FAITHFUL DEPARTED

During the course of an illness, one may be visited many times by a pastoral minister or lay volunteer bringing Holy Communion to the home and praying with the sick. Before a major surgery, or when one is in failing health, they may also receive the sacrament of the anointing of the sick. Many are afraid of this, thinking it is a sure sign they are about to die. But remember, sacraments are for the living. One may be anointed multiple times in life.

In pre-Vatican II days, the concept of "Extreme Unction" or "Last Rites" was prevalent as the only time one was anointed. Then, one made a last confession, received communion, and was anointed on their deathbed. When someone is ill, they may be visited by a pastoral care worker or volunteer, or by the priest, who may anoint them. The introduction to the anointing of the sick states: "The priest should ensure that the abuse of delaying the sacrament does not occur, and that the celebration takes place while the sick person is capable of active participation" and that "those needing the sacrament should seek it at the beginning of a serious illness" (99). It is preferable to anoint someone who has the wherewithal to understand they are receiving the sacrament, but if not, God's grace still prevails.

The *Catechism* reminds us, "The Eucharist should always be the last sacrament of the earthly journey, the 'viaticum' for 'passing over' to Eternal life" (1517). In the absence of a priest, a lay person may give someone this final communion but may not anoint them or hear their confession and give absolution.

There may be a Catholic hospital chaplain on staff or on call at your local hospital, or perhaps the priests in the area have a rotation system where each takes different days or nights of the week. Often, though, hospital staff may be calling around scrambling to find any priest to come anoint a person. There are times when someone may be dead on arrival, or when a family calls the parish because a loved one has just passed away. At those times, the priest may come and pray with the family, and many will find comfort in that, but he cannot anoint the deceased, though some will do what is call a "conditional anointing."

However, there are beautiful "Commendation of the Dying" prayers, as well as the "Prayers for the Dead" found in the *Order of Christian Funerals* (OCF). If the priest knows the family well, being there at this time will surely be a comfort to them. When a priest or pastoral minister is able to come and visit and pray with the family, it may help a family that is less connected feel closer to the church, and it may also provide a sense of the person's life, and their family, so that the priest and staff are better able to minister to them. At this time, the family may be overwhelmed and not know what to do next; so helping them address this will help lessen their confusion.

It is good to recall that the priest must do the anointing, or reconciliation, but any pastoral care worker or Minister of Communion may visit with the sick, or offer communion and prayers with the dead. Perhaps there is someone on your staff assigned these tasks, and they can steer the family in the right direction.

WHOM DO I CALL FIRST?

Hopefully, your parish has a good working relationship with local funeral homes. Often it is the funeral home that notifies the parish of a death, but it is usually better if the family calls the church before going to visit the home. This way staff can be aware of the death to add the name to general intercessions and parish bulletins, and begin making plans for the impending funeral. Sometimes the logistics of getting family members, priest, musicians, and the mortuary together are really difficult. Once upon a time it might have been simple to say, "Mom died, and we want to have her funeral on Thursday at 11 AM," but with the shortage of priests, and the frequent clustering of parishes, there are fewer people to cover a much larger area.

Often, families end up meeting with the funeral home before they come in and plan the funeral liturgy, and the home is rushing to get the obituary into the paper. Sometimes decisions are made about what the services will look like without consulting the parish, and this can make it more difficult for those meeting to plan the funeral. For example, the family may be planning to have a visitation before church in the narthex, and no Vigil service, yet they have four people who want to speak about the deceased. This can be problematic, and would be a situation where a Vigil service may have been very beneficial. It is wise to provide families with some outline of the funeral process, so that they can make planning decisions that they feel good about. There are times when people do start out by calling the funeral home, and surely, the two make it work, but encourage your people to contact your parish first.

UNDERSTANDING THE STRUCTURE OF THE FUNERAL RITUAL

The Vigil

Ideally, the Rite of Christian Burial should be a threefold rite. There should be a Rite of Reception and Vigil for the Deceased, frequently taking place the night before at the funeral home or church itself. Usually what happens is that there is a brief service at the end of a visitation period. According to the *Order of Christian Funerals*, "The vigil in the form of the liturgy of the word consists of the introductory rites, the liturgy of the word, the prayer of intercession, and a concluding rite" (57).

This is the first stage of grief for many who, perhaps, see the body and casket or urn for the first time. It is also a time to greet and hug and share tears and laughter. For those unable to attend the funeral, it is a chance to share their respects with the family. It is also a time when many non-Catholic friends frequently come because they are more comfortable with a visitation than with the funeral liturgy. In many cultures the vigil or wake used to last several days and was frequently held in the home. This was a very healthy part of the grieving process that we have lost in many ways.

Being connected electronically also changes things. Sometimes instead of waiting in line to sign a guest book, people offer their condolences at a website set up by the funeral home or at legacy.com. Similarly, since many people post information about a loved one's death on social media, they may be getting notes from hundreds of people offering pictures, stories, and sympathies. This is especially true in times of tragedies. Often someone will start a GoFundMe page to ask for financial help for the funeral. It is also not uncommon for obituaries to request that in lieu of flowers, donations may be made to the funeral expenses, the Cancer Society, the local parish, or a charity of their choice.

The Vigil itself is usually presided over by a priest or deacon, but it easily could be a Sister, or a commissioned, trained lay person. Sometimes, the Vigil takes the shape of the Rosary instead of a word service, or groups like the Knights of Columbus or a women's altar guild will do a Rosary or a prayer service before the formal Vigil begins.

This is also a place for family members to share their remarks of remembrance or a eulogy. In fact it is more appropriate to do so now than on the day of the funeral itself. Sometimes the person leading the service will open it up to remarks from the floor, or this is the place where all the grandchildren can "share something special about grandpa," etc. One of the beautiful things about a visitation, especially away from the church, is that it is a fine place to play the Elvis songs grandma so loved, or something else that is special, quirky, and a beloved part of the departed. Put simply, the Vigil and visitation are very much about the deceased, and there is a simple ritual in place, but there is also some leeway in how it is celebrated.

Due to busy schedules, and the economics involved, there are many times when families no longer opt for a separate Vigil. Sometimes it depends on whether they have talked to the funeral home or the church first. It is becoming very common for there to be a one- or two-hour visitation at the church before the funeral, which may then be a day or evening funeral.

The difficult thing about this is that then people try and put everything into the funeral—the poems, the fishing stories, the favorite song from high school, each child sharing memories of Dad. (This author was at a funeral once where four children each told the same story of a toy airplane and took over twenty minutes to do so.) Add to that the K of C still wanting to get their Rosary or prayer service in, and it can become a very messy rite of redundant and combined rituals and non-Catholic things. It is always challenging when we mix devotional prayer (the Rosary) and liturgical prayer (word service). This is similar to the growing number of elements that people try and throw into a wedding today, just because they saw it someplace else or read about it on Pinterest.

Sometimes, this is where the hard part of balancing pastoral and professional comes in. It is our job to know the rites and rituals and keep to them as best we can. In reading obituaries, it becomes very obvious that many people are not religious and are inventing their own funerals or making things up along the way. They are often called "Celebrations of Life," and many times people want to bring this title into the Catholic liturgy, but the funeral liturgy is not so much about the deceased. We can lose the focus that this is a Mass of Resurrection. The message is that Jesus Christ died and rose again so that we might have eternal life. We are there to pray for the person who died.

The Funeral Mass

The Rite reminds us:

> At the funeral liturgy the community gathers with the family and friends of the deceased to give praise and thanks to God for Christ's victory over sin and death, to commend the deceased to God's tender mercy and compassion, and to seek strength in the proclamation of the paschal mystery. Through the Holy Spirit the community is joined together in faith as one Body in Christ to reaffirm in sign and symbol, word and gesture that each believer through baptism shares in Christ's death and resurrection and can look to the day when all the elect will be raised up and united in the kingdom of light and peace. ▪ **OCF 129**

If we can understand this ourselves, and help those we are working with to enter into this glorious mystery, the funeral will be all the richer for that—by virtue of the very rite itself, without adding all the extras. Celebrate the life with more shared memories at a meal afterward.

Funerals may not be celebrated Holy Thursday morning or throughout the Paschal Triduum, the Sundays of Advent, Lent, and Easter, or on Holy Days of Obligation (*General Instruction of the Roman Missal* [GIRM], 380). While a funeral may technically be celebrated on a Sunday of Ordinary Time, very few priests are willing to do that. Adding this on top of the weekend's roster of Masses is extremely demanding on them physically and spiritually. Technically, a Sunday service could only be one without a Mass. Rather than get into the minute details, most parishes simply say "no" to Sundays. Besides the parish difficulties, it would be very hard to work with a cemetery on that day, so burial would have to take place later.

Visitation

Many times there is a visitation at church prior to the funeral. Depending on parish tradition, size of funeral, and architecture, this may take place in a gathering space or narthex, or in the body of the church itself. It is important to have a clear understanding of what may or may not be allowed in these spaces.

Picture boards, florals, PowerPoint videos, and other memorabilia come to mind here. It is helpful to have a clear policy in writing as to what your parish or diocese allows. Make sure that you have the same materials posted on your parish website, as some people will go there first looking for information. If this is included in writing in your planning materials it will help you in difficult situations so that you do not have to make a decision on the fly. If the visitation is in the church itself, some of these materials may need to be removed before the liturgy, depending on the liturgical season or the policies of the parish.

Many churches clearly state that the flowers and environment in the church are not to be disturbed. Some may suggest that a few bouquets may remain in the church for the liturgy, while in other parishes they must be removed beforehand. (*Note:* The liturgical season may also play a factor in this, e.g., flowers in Lent.) One parish may welcome flowers and plants from funerals as donations, and another may say "please remove them all." Things like that may depend on the pastor involved, or whether your church has three funerals a month or five funerals a week.

THE FUNERAL MASS

People can be easily overwhelmed by explanations of the funeral liturgy. A simple way to describe it is, "The beginning and end are a little more complex, but the Liturgy of the Word and the Eucharist are the same," or help put them at ease by saying, "It doesn't matter if you don't understand what comes next. We do, and we'll help you along."

While you may want to put their minds at ease, some persons are more detail oriented, or will want to return to the information another time to prepare themselves mentally. It might be a good idea to have another sheet explaining frequently asked questions or "What to Expect at a Catholic Funeral Mass." I do not like to discuss parish and musician fees during a planning session. Usually the mortuary will take care of that, but it is good to include that information somewhere so that people may have access to it in advance.

The Funeral Mass—Introductory Rites

This is the outline given for the Introductory Rites. They are meant to be brief.

GREETING—These begin with a simple formula. This is not a chatty "how do you do" or "welcome to the parish." It is scripted in the rite. There are four texts given in OCF 277.

SPRINKLING WITH HOLY WATER AND/OR BRIEF ADDRESS—OCF 278 offers this beautiful prayer for those baptized: "In the waters of baptism N. died with Christ and rose with him to new life. May he/she now share with him eternal glory." It is important to note this is not a time for everyone in the church to sprinkle the casket or urn. That is a tradition that can take place at two other times. Holy water may be available by a prie-dieu during the visitation, or family members and friends may bless with holy water after the Rite of Final Commendation.

Placing of the Pall—OCF 279. This is optional and depends on local custom, but may be done by family, friends, or the funeral home. The pall is typically white and is a beautiful symbol of baptism. There is no formal text to accompany this action, but it is helpful if the priest offers a word of explanation, especially if this is taking place in the back of church, because many people cannot see and are relying on the commentary to participate. It is also a brief teaching moment. (*Note:* In the appendix on cremation, OCF 434 clearly states that the covering with pall is to be omitted.)

Entrance Procession

Placing of Christian Symbols—OCF 281 invites, "A symbol of the Christian life, such as a cross may be carried in procession, then placed on the coffin, either in silence or as a specific text from the rite is said."

Opening Prayer—Now we are back into the familiar territory of the liturgy, as this is a prayer straight from the *Roman Missal* in the format people are accustomed to. There are different prayers for celebrating funerals of children, or the unbaptized as well.

While these elements of the Introductory Rites are listed in a clear order in the OCF, what may actually happen could look a bit different depending on the traditions in your parish. Often these center around architecture. As Professor James White taught me in grad school, "Liturgy is ritual, but architecture is king!" meaning the rite and the rubrics may say one thing, but you have to make it work in the building you are in. Several factors come into play here. Where did the visitation take place? Is the casket or urn coming forward in procession, or is it already in place? Will family members be accompanying the procession or are they already seated?

For example, in the parish I serve, it is different if there is a casket or cremated remains present.

With a casket, the procession begins in the back with the welcome and the sprinkling, and then the entrance song is sung while it comes forward. With an urn, though the rite permits it, our parish policy is that it is not carried in procession, but placed in the ossuary beforehand.

So in a funeral liturgy with the urn/ossuary, the liturgy actually begins with the opening hymn and procession, and then the rite of reception and sprinkling with holy water takes place once they have reached the sanctuary. Similarly, you may have to adapt that order to your own situation.

Entrance Antiphon—One thing to note is that the OCF says nothing about Entrance and Communion Antiphons, but the Roman Missal itself provides a couple of options for these. Consider reciting or singing them as a regular part of the liturgy. It could easily take place before the greeting.

THE FUNERAL MASS—LITURGY OF THE WORD

Scripture Readings—Readings from the Old and New Testament are provided. Typically there will be one of each, but OCF 283 reminds that "depending on pastoral situations either one or two readings may be read before the gospel reading." In the case of two readings, there is an Old Testament and New Testament reading, unless we are in the Easter Season, in which case there are some New Testament options that may be used as the first reading. There is always a gospel reading.

Sometimes the challenge is that people come in with three gospels, or a couple of psalms or something else. That is when it is important for the staff to step in and help straighten things out. As OCF 344 reminds us, "in consultation with the family and close friends, the minister chooses the texts that most closely reflect the particular circumstances and the needs of the mourners."

No matter how you "package" the Scriptures, it may be hard to find just the right ones; it will take good discussion and listening. It is interesting to see how other authors have tried to do this.

In his 1987 book *Funeral Liturgies*, Irish priest Flor McCarthy creates "sets" of readings, e.g., an Old Testament, New Testament, and gospel reading that fit together, along with a sample homily to go with it. While this may be a helpful tool for the pastor for reflection, or for a Vigil service, I don't think it is something you would want to present to the families.

In a more recent attempt, Father Paul Turner creates thematic indexes of the Scripture readings in his book *Light in the Darkness: Preparing Better Catholic Funerals*. This is a more helpful approach, but what they both tell me is that the person working with the family to plan the funeral rite must have an intimate knowledge of the funeral rite, and of the Scriptures involved. That way, you can simply make the loose association to a reading when talking with the family. (The same is true for hymnody and making the right suggestions.)

The Responsorial Psalm—Frequently, people say things like, "We want the Twenty-third Psalm recited by my uncle." It is important to explain that it is sung as a responsorial psalm within the context of the liturgy. One can sometimes defuse a situation by either offering a sung version of the psalm, or suggesting that in lieu of remarks of remembrance, or as part of them, the psalm be recited in whole before the liturgy begins, or it could be put on a prayer card, or recited together at the cemetery. Learning how to gently tell people "no" and moving them on to another idea is truly an art in compassion and care.

The Homily—A brief homily is given after the gospel reading. Again, the homily is based upon the readings and our hope in the resurrection. It may mention the individual who has died or offer connecting points about their life and the Scriptures, but this is not the time for a eulogy.

The General Intercessions—OCF 285 provides intercessions but says that they may be adapted or new ones composed. Think strongly before you veer from them, though. There is a lot of powerful resurrection theology in them.

THE FUNERAL MASS—LITURGY OF THE EUCHARIST

The Liturgy of the Eucharist takes place in the normal fashion. There are particular prefaces to be used for this. Sometimes, family members assist as Extraordinary Ministers, but if so, they should be practicing Catholics familiar with this role. Often, before the distribution of communion, it is helpful if the priest explains how it is to take place, e.g., "We will distribute the Body and Blood of Christ to the right side of the church first. Afterward, I will move to the left-hand side. You may receive communion if you are a Catholic in good standing, or you may come forward with your arms crossed to receive a blessing if you will not be receiving communion. If not, you are welcome to remain in the pew. Thank you."

THE FUNERAL MASS—FINAL COMMENDATION

Remarks of Remembrance—After Communion, there may be remarks of remembrance offered, though I recommend moving them to before the liturgy begins. In any instance, have clear, concise instructions on what is expected and allowed, e.g., "one page, typed; or three to five minutes."

Invitation to Prayer—There is a formal prayer offered, followed by silence.

The rite is rather nebulous about when the casket or urn is to be sprinkled with holy water or incensed. It suggests it may take place before or during the Song of Farewell. This is an easy place for the priest and musicians to falter if they are not on the same wavelength. I have found it very helpful when the priest offers an introduction to the Song of Farewell. Just add a simple note or sticky tack to your ritual book saying something like this: "In a moment, as we incense the body of N., we will recall that the incense is a symbol of our prayers rising to heaven [a reference to Psalm 141], and accompanying him/her on his/her journey. Please join us in singing the Song of Farewell found on the back of your order of worship."

Song of Farewell—This is a frequently misunderstood part of the liturgy. There are times when people just put in any song they want or see this as a place for a solo. However, if one looks at OCF 292, there are clearly specific texts called for. Some of the Catholic publishers do a disservice to families by providing other contemporary texts that are just songs of grief or mourning. They may be beautiful, but they do not replace the song of farewell. It is also an important spot to have everybody praying. By the use of a very simple tune, such as the "Old Hundredth" or "Londonderry Air" settings, you will easily get active participation. Or choose a version that is sung in a responsorial format.

Procession to the Place of Committal—Again, a careful look at 294 of the Rite suggests a particular text: "May the angels lead you into Paradise," the traditional "*In Paradisum*." Sadly, this whole beautiful setting has frequently been lost to simply singing a "closing song" or a "recessional hymn."

As perhaps a way of trying to return to the rite itself, but offering some sort of compromise, the latest version of the funeral planning book and materials at my parish lists *In Paradisum* (*May the Angels Lead You*) as the recessional. If the family still wants "Amazing Grace" or another hymn and they weren't able to fit it into the places offered within the liturgy, it will take place after this formal recessional song.

(*Note:* Any time you change a parish tradition or policy, it is good to inform your congregation through the use of a bulletin article, website blurb, or in one of the homilies, so that people may have an understanding of it in advance. The transition will take a while, but soon it will be just "the way things are." One needs a very strong cantor and/or choir to make something like that song work.)

RITE OF COMMITTAL

The third portion of the funeral is the Committal. These brief prayers are usually said at the cemetery itself, though they may be recited in the church after the funeral liturgy. Or, if the burial is at a distant location, sometimes funeral home personnel can take care of this rite. Geography is often a factor. Little local churches used to have their cemetery adjacent to the parish, and the pallbearers could carry a casket there, or the casket would be on a horse-drawn trailer or in a hearse. But now, the cemetery may be miles away. Often, the timing of this is determined by the place of burial itself; e.g., they may charge you more money to have the burial after 1:00 PM on a Saturday, so this timing becomes a key factor in all the planning. Similarly, a funeral home would charge more to bring the casket over to the church for visitation Thursday night, and again for the funeral itself on Friday morning. Sadly, economics are often a huge factor in the decisions people make around funerals, and it is important always to be sensitive to them.

While we must be attentive to church rites, guidelines, and structure, one must always do so within a pastoral mindset. The funeral is a chance to provide witness and evangelization to those who have fallen away or who are not in the church. How you treat them will make a lot of difference on whether you will ever see them in your church again!

While the rite itself is very brief, there may be some variations in the way the graveyard service itself is carried out. For example, people may be invited to sprinkle the casket or urn with holy water. It is a time for one last prayer and respect. Others may offer everyone a rose or flower from the casket spray to take with them as a memento. In some places, people stay and sing as the casket is lowered into the ground. When I was in the monastery, we sang Taizé hymns like "Jesus Remember Me" and "Surrexit Christus" at this time. Still others may have bagpipes play or release balloons in the air. What is important is to help the family realize where the rite begins and ends.

FUNERAL LITURGY OUTSIDE THE MASS

We discussed the Funeral Mass of Christian Burial, but the funeral rite also provides for a simpler word service, which primarily takes place at the funeral home. This is often employed in mixed-church families or lapsed Catholic situations, or for other pastoral reasons. It must be made clear that no Liturgy of the Eucharist will be celebrated. Again, there are sometimes times and reasons for these services, but convenience for the family should not be the whole basis for this decision. These services are often very minimal, with priest or deacon presiding, and either no music or canned recorded music from the funeral home itself. But there is no reason live music cannot be a part of the service, and is to be encouraged.

MILITARY HONORS

When one has served in the active military, they are entitled to military honors at their funeral. This will likely consist of members of the local VFW or American Legion post being present during the visitation. Sometimes they take turns standing at honor at the casket. The coffin will be draped in a flag during this time, but that flag must be removed before the liturgy begins.

After the funeral itself, there will probably be "Taps" and a rifle salute. Again, depending on timing and geography, this may take place outside of the church before the casket is placed in the hearse, or may take place at the cemetery itself. Usually the funeral home will take care of contacting the organization. (*Note:* This is different from the funeral of an active military person, which is discussed elsewhere in this book.)

A PLANNING GUIDE

I have heard many horror stories at the time of funerals, when families have been turned loose with a popular funeral book that includes readings and some prayer options but provides little helpful information, and simply told, "Let us know what you want." That approach is useful to no one. Reading through all the Scriptures suggested for funerals can be an overwhelming task in itself. Then, if you add all the options for opening prayers, prayers over the gifts, Eucharistic prayers, and several options for intercessions, it becomes ridiculous. There are some details the family doesn't need to make decisions on—they should be made by the priest and the staff. All the people need to worry about are the Scriptures, the music, and the ministries. Even that is more than some families can handle, and you will need to break the tasks down for people. No two situations are alike.

Provide people with a clear, concise outline of the funeral (Appendix I), and another with blanks to fill in for all the options they may have, e.g., Scriptures, music, and ministers (Appendix II). In the booklet created for my parish, there are sections for Old Testament, New Testament, and Gospel. We start by explaining that we will need three readings, like at a Sunday Mass. In the booklet there is a summary page for the Old Testament readings, which provides the Scripture citations and a brief one-sentence synopsis of the reading, followed by the page number that the actual Scripture citation is on. (For example: Job 19:1, 23-37 "I know that my Vindicator (Redeemer) lives." page 37.) So when reading a synopsis strikes a chord with someone, they may actually read the Scripture choice and see if it fits. There are similar selections for the New Testament and Gospel. (*Note well:* Before you publish something online using readings from the Lectionary, it is necessary to get copyright permission from the USCCB. One can also find a link to all the Lectionary Scripture readings for funerals at www.usccb.org/prayer-and-worship/bereavement-and-funerals/index.cfm.) The beauty of having the readings online or in a PDF format is that you may provide them to someone for distant planning. Recently I sat with a woman in Wisconsin, and her sister called in from Florida and followed along in our booklet, which we had emailed out earlier. It was a great solution to a distance problem. One could also easily Skype, FaceTime, or use any number of media platforms to bridge the miles.

While the actual *Order of Christian Funerals* contains the Scriptures to be used for liturgies, through many years of this ministry we have discovered that there are times when it is hard to find something in the official OCF list of readings to provide comfort or to match a certain situation. In these instances we went back to the Bible and found readings beyond those suggested in the Rite itself. There is precedent for this. I kept track of readings that we used in these situations and created an expanded list (Appendix III). It continues to grow and evolve. A planning book could offer many of these alternate readings so that one does not have to go grasping at straws.

In cases of preplanning, many times it seems those who have been dealing with a long illness or nearing death have found having the booklet of readings to pray with a powerful source of strength and hope as well.

FUNERAL MUSIC

Earlier, we alluded to "cookie-cutter funerals" with the same music used every time. Experience has shown that this is often the case because these popular songs were the first that came to mind. However, when provided with alternatives, families often make other choices. Go through your parish hymnal and resources and make lists of songs that may be appropriate for prelude, entrance chant, offertory, communion, thanksgiving, and closing. Your hymnal may have some helper guides and topics, such as grief, mourning, comfort, and resurrection, to offer guidance. With many hymnals under one copyright license this should also expand the choices you can provide (Appendix IV).

Then, add additional seasonal and Marian columns. There are many beautiful hymns that reflect the time of the liturgical year—which needs to be considered as well. For example, in Advent, celebrate a joyous Mass of Resurrection by ending with an upbeat "Soon and Very Soon We are Going to See the King," or "The King Shall Come When Morning Dawns."

One may never get over the sorrow of losing a loved one during the Christmas season, so isn't it better to embrace it? "Good Christian Friends" reminds us "Now ye need not fear the grave, Jesus Christ was born to save." Look at the text to "Hark the Herald Angels Sing," which proclaims, "Mild he lays his glory by, born that we no more may die, born to raise us from the earth, born to give us second birth." "Silent Night" calls us to "Sleep in heavenly peace."

Easter songs are wonderful in the season, but I suggest they are also appropriate throughout the year. (But be aware of Alleluias in Lent!) "Alleluia the Strife is Oe'r" is especially meaningful when someone has overcome a long illness, or "I know That My Redeemer Lives" is a direct tie to the Job reading. Similarly, if someone has a Marian devotion, one version of "Hail Holy Queen" says, "And when our life breath leaves us, show us the face of Jesus..." (OCP).

Do include a notation in your planning book that all music within the liturgy is to be live and not recorded. “Recorded music lacks the authenticity provided by a living liturgical assembly gathered for the Sacred Liturgy” (*Sing to the Lord*, 93). Putting this in writing ahead of time will often save hard feelings and disappointment.

I spoke of this before, but friends, go back to your funeral rite, and reread the section on “the Song of Farewell.” You will note that it is a very specific text. “Saints of God, come to his/her aid…” (OCF 292). There are a couple of other choices listed in the appendix to the rite (OCF 403). Sadly, many parishes will just see this as another slot for a song or a solo. It is a communal prayer. Respect the rite.

In the funeral planning book that we use, I have divided hymns into simple suggestions of entrance, psalms, offertory, communion, and recessional to help people know where to place the music. I have a note that one’s choices are not limited to these suggestions, but they are a good starter.

While working on this manuscript, I went to the website of a large metropolitan Catholic parish. Besides the divisions I’ve mentioned, they actually had an “Other” section, with links to YouTube for most of these songs:

Aquarius (from *Hair*)
Angel (Sarah McLachlan)
Ave Maria (Bach-Gounod, not in hymnals)
Ave Maria (Schubert, not in hymnals)
Blue Skies (Irving Berlin)
Breathe (Michael W. Smith)
Canon in D (Johann Pachelbel, Dona Nobis Pacem mix)
Con Te Partiro—Time to Say Goodbye (Andrea Bocelli and Sarah Brightman, not in hymnals)
Come Now Almighty King (Italian Hymn)
The Dance (Garth Brooks)

Eternal Father, Strong to Save (Navy Hymn)
Go in Peace (Hart, Liles)
God Will Wipe Away Every Tear
Hallelujah (L. Cohen)
Hail Mary, Gentle Woman
He Lives in You (from *The Lion King*)
Husky Fight Song
I Can Only Imagine (Mercy Me)
I Am the Bread of Life (Toolan)
I Will Remember You (Sarah McLachlan)
In the Garden (not in hymnals)
Jesu, Joy of Man's Desiring
Lord of the Dance
Lullabye—Goodnight My Angel (Billy Joel)
My Sweet Lord (George Harrison)
My Way (Frank Sinatra singing)
Night and Day
Ombra mai fu (from Handel's *Xerxes*, sung at many Italian funerals, I've learned)
Panis Angelicus (Franck, solo song, not in hymnals)
Pie Jesu (Andrew Lloyd Webber, duet not in hymnals)
Prayer of St. Francis
Precious Lord, Take My Hand (sung here by Elvis)
Solace (Scott Joplin, piano solo)
Simple Gifts
Somewhere over the Rainbow
The Wind Beneath My Wings
You Raise Me Up (Josh Groban)

I saw this list and thought, "Why would you try and encourage anyone to do some of these songs? This is exactly the sort of bad theology and liturgy we should be trying to avoid!" There are some things on the list like "Prayer of Saint Francis," or "I am the Bread of Life," that are totally appropriate, and "Panis Angelicus," "Ave Maria," and "Hail Mary Gentle Woman" are songs that are not uncommon to be at a funeral as a thanksgiving piece, but I surely would not give someone a list like this, or put it out on the website where people can make decisions without discussing it for any pastoral considerations.

Are there exceptions? Always. But they should be that and not the norm. For example, there was a little old man who spent fifty years playing in a polka band. When the final song was complete, and the funeral was officially "done," we played a tape of "And When I Get to Heaven I'll Dance the Polka." Or someone might have "Notre Dame, Our Mother" sung after communion. Each case must be handled with prayer and delicacy.

OTHER ELEMENTS

Some other things that you might wish to include in a planning guide or a funeral workshop would be Frequently Asked Questions and a Glossary of terms that are common to your parish or your region (Appendix VI). While the rites are universal, it still seems that there are some things that vary by geographic region or by diocese.

There are some things not related to the liturgy but very important to people. You may wish to provide forms for them at your workshops, or have people available to talk about topics like Living Wills and DNR policies and Organ Donor Information (may vary by state), buying plots at Catholic or local cemeteries, welcoming local funeral homes to join you at your presentation so people may have a chance to visit with them or pick up information afterwards, or including someone from the parish finance office to talk about remembering the parish in wills and life insurance policies. It is not easy to wade through the ethical and spiritual dilemmas around end of life decisions. Here is a good resource to help: https://www.ncbcenter.org/publications/end-life-guide/.

The Catholic Health Association of the United States has information on advanced directives. Here is a link to their pamphlet, which answers many questions (it is also available in printed form): https://www.chausa.org/docs/default-source/ethics/3059-cha_end-of-life-guide_ad_lores.pdf?sfvrsn=2 (4455 Woodson Road, St. Louis MO 63134-3797; 314-253-3458; fax 314-427-0029).

Encourage families to talk about their wishes. Perhaps someone wishes to be an organ donor, or another firmly believes in DNR. How can you know these details if you don't talk about them? Conversations may be awkward but will save a lot of emotional and spiritual anguish in the long run.

Don't expect people to fill out their information right then during your presentation, but presenting information about advance directives can be helpful on many levels. Often a middle-aged person attends with their elderly parent, and this is the first time that they have been able to openly talk about death and the parent's wishes. This has opened the door for many family communications.

Frequently, those who attend a workshop schedule a follow-up, one-on-one appointment, at which time they can be guided through the process at their own pace. Other times, they may fill the forms out at home in privacy. In my office I have a file of funeral plans, and I suggest that people give a copy to their families, and place them with their funeral home plans in a safe or safety deposit box, or other important place. One family found their mom's plans in the family Bible. As a liturgist, I have found it a powerful experience when someone brings in a planning sheet written in their mom's handwriting and I know that I can be part of honoring and respecting this woman's wishes. Recently a man died, and his wife came in to meet about the funeral. She brought the guide from a workshop she had attended five years earlier, and it was clear it was a well-thumbed and prayed-over document. It made the planning go much more smoothly.

One should know that there are times when the plans may not be able to be executed one hundred percent accurately. For example, the family may have chosen an "Alleluia" song and it is Lent, or a niece chosen to read the first reading may not be able to attend the funeral when the time comes. But by offering some form of preplanning, you are at the very least doing justice to the person as best you can.

CHAPTER THREE

Toward a Better Understanding of Cremation

BY FAR THE MOST NUMBER OF QUESTIONS AND THE AREA MOST IMPORTANT TO PROVIDE CLEAR INFORMATION IMBUED BY A PASTORAL UNDERSTANDING IS THE AREA OF CREMATION. Because of the intricacies of this subject, and the many emotions that surround it, we are giving it its own chapter.

If you ask "Does the church allow cremation?" the nutshell answer is "yes," but there are many more considerations and nuances that should be addressed. For many centuries the church did not allow cremation, except for extreme situations like plague or war. The theology or idea was that the body was to be buried whole, because, as we profess in the Creed, "Jesus will come in glory to judge the living and the dead" and at that time a glorified, resurrected body will be reunited with the soul of the faithful departed. In the nineteenth century, many seeking cremation were denying this resurrection of the body, as did earlier pagan cremations.

In 1983 the new *Code of Canon Law* said "The Church earnestly recommends that the pious custom of burying the bodies of the dead be observed; it does not, however, forbid cremation unless it has been chosen for reasons (that) are contrary to Christian teaching" (1176.3). Similarly, in 1997 the OCF came out with an appendix on cremation. That appendix stated clearly that cremation is allowed, but it is greatly preferred that the body be there whole for the Mass of Christian Burial and that cremation take place afterward (OCF 413-414). It acknowledged in paragraph 415 that there are *extraordinary* times when the body may not be present, and that there is a need for "pastoral sensitivity" in these situations.

Never in their wildest dreams did anyone think that cremation would become the norm, but according to the National Funeral Directors Association, "50.2 percent of Americans chose cremation in 2016, up from 48.5 percent in 2015, while 43.5 percent of Americans opted for burial, down from 45.4 percent in 2015." In the next twenty years that figure is expected to rise to an over seventy percent cremation rate.

There are many factors involved in these changes, but frequent ones include less religion in households, increasing mobility, and the cost of funerals. To buy a casket, embalm, and pay for a vault and graveside services can easily run seven thousand to ten thousand dollars these days. Cremation can cost as little as a third of that. In understanding this, the United States Conference of Catholic Bishops (USCCB) released a statement in their Liturgy Newsletter and website: (www.usccb.org/prayer-and-worship/bereavement-and-funerals/cremation-and-funerals.cfm). It calls for a much more pastoral sensitivity to families around the subject of cremation.

Here is a place where having a good working relationship with your local funeral homes is important. Have a meeting with them and explore options. Explain the Catholic desire to have the body present, and ask them if there is a way that they can help. For example, can the deceased's body be present at a funeral without embalming, or is possible to get a rental casket?

Perhaps your parish could consider investing in a rental casket to help keep costs down. (*Reminder:* This is all good information to be shared at that funeral planning workshop.)

But remember, if someone chooses to have their loved one cremated, it is important to note that "the cremated remains of a body should be treated with the same respect given to the human body from which they come" (OCF 417). The rite goes on to say that holy water may be used, and the Rite of Committal takes place as well. When talking about respect, paragraph 417 continues:

> This includes the use of a worthy vessel to contain the ashes, the manner in which they are carried, the care and attention to appropriate placement and transport, and the final disposition. The cremated remains should be buried in a grave or entombed in a mausoleum or columbarium. The practice of scattering cremated remains on the sea, from the air, or on the ground, or keeping cremated remains in the home of a relative or friend of the deceased are not the reverent disposition that the church requires...

There are two separate issues involved here: worthy vessels and appropriate treatment of the remains. Let us address each of them.

In recent years, the idea of "appropriate vessels" has varied widely. In a thirty-second Google search for funeral urns, I found many urns that I would deem appropriate or traditional, and sold by everyone from Amazon to Walmart. One can spend twenty dollars or two thousand dollars on an urn. But disturbingly enough, there were also several "novelty" urns, such as one shaped like a man's toolbox, a golf ball, a little log cabin, or an hourglass where you could watch the remains as "sand" moving back and forth. I have also seen examples where Dad was brought to church inside a Crown Royal bottle. These cases become problematic. OCF 434 notes that a pall is not to be used when cremation has taken place, so what do you do? Clearly these novelty urns may reflect the individual's hobbies but have no dignity for the funeral ritual itself.

Our solution was to get a beautiful wooden ossuary that is used for all funerals. During the visitation (which is usually in the narthex) the urn may be visible as always, but shortly before the service the funeral home places it in the ossuary in church. Meyer-Vogelpohl Church Supply does make a handcrafted ossuary on a stand, and St. Meinrad Abbey makes one that is more like a bier that may be carried in procession by four people. When we first got this, we talked with all the funeral homes. When they meet with families, they explain that this is how it is displayed in church during the funeral, and it has never been an issue. There are some things that aren't up to the people. Set parish policies and abide by them.

The second issue was the appropriate treatment of remains. It takes much education in continued bulletin articles and homilies for your parish to understand that they may not scatter the ashes and to understand the theology of the whole body and the resurrection. One frequently hears about families dividing ashes up between the kids, or someone requesting to be spread at their favorite places in life. Besides being theologically wrong, a priest I knew used to try and help families understand by saying something like, "Don't spread the ashes. It may seem like the right thing to do now, but down the road, you will be struck with the emptiness of having nothing. It is important to inter the ashes, so that you do have a place to go." It was much more palatable than saying "You can't do that!" Another viable option of interring ashes in a columbarium is this: If the family had to move, there might be the possibility of securing another spot for the ashes, close to where they are living now, and they would still have a proper resting place. Some new churches are adding columbaria right on the church property.

Besides spreading ashes, there are a couple of new-age trends that are rather alarming. People are getting jewelry made with a portion of the ashes in them, so that their loved one may always be a part of them. One can pay to have ashes scattered in space, or even loaded into shotgun shells. Or ashes are being spun into glass, which is then made into hand-blown vases. None of these forms of dealing with the cremated remains is appropriate. They are gimmicks.

If someone has already done something like this, it would be good to convince them to bury anything left in hallowed ground. Again, it is important to find a pastoral way to have these discussions about cremation. It is indeed a touchy subject. You don't want anybody to feel like they are going to hell because of the way they took care of their husband, but do everything you can to make sure the deceased is in sacred earth.

Probably the most common misunderstanding is the spouse who leaves the urn on their dresser at home. Perhaps they are waiting until they themselves die and will be interred together; perhaps they just can't face letting go of their loved ones; or perhaps burial is a financial hardship. The USCCB newsletter mentioned earlier suggests that parishes or dioceses may offer a chance for people to bring their loved ones to be buried together in a communal plot around All Souls Day. This may not be something done every year but may become an occasional event.

In the town I serve, the parishes got together and did this for the Year of Mercy in 2015. One of the Corporal Works of Mercy is to bury the dead. There were a couple of bulletin columns explaining what was being offered, it was spoken about from the pulpit, and local ads were taken out in the city newspaper. The people simply needed to contact the parish office and make arrangements to be part of this, at no cost to them. The parish cemetery donated the plots, and a headstone was purchased with the names of all the deceased. A beautiful, simple committal was given, and many people were relieved of a burden they had been carrying for some time.

In 2016, the Vatican issued *Ad resurgendum cum Christo*, which again stated the importance of Christian burial so that "every appearance of pantheism, naturalism, or nihilism be avoided" (p. 7). It also speaks out against new things like the biodegradable burial pods that turn a person's body into a tree,

> By burying the bodies of the faithful, the Church confirms her faith in the resurrection of the body, and intends to show the great dignity of the human body as an integral part of the human person whose body forms part of their identity. She cannot, therefore, condone attitudes or permit rites that involve erroneous ideas about death, such as considering death as the definitive annihilation of the person, or the movement of fusion with Mother Nature or the universe, or as a stage in the cycle of regeneration, or as the definitive liberation from the "prison" of the body. ■ ***Ad resurgendum cum Christo*, 3**

The document even goes so far as to say that if a person is insistent on scattering ashes they may be denied a Christian burial.

This author just read a very disturbing article that said funeral homes are starting to preserve the skin of the deceased by removing an area with a tattoo, processing the skin like leather, and then framing it for families (https://www.menshealth.com/style/a20965680/

save-my-ink-forever-tattoos/). This lack of respect for the human body is what the church is trying to avoid.

Another growing trend in some regions of the United States involves no longer placing the deceased person in a casket. Rather, funeral planners are setting up elaborate displays where the deceased may be sitting or standing, engaging in lifelike activities. One woman was sitting at a table with her drink in one hand and an unlit cigarette in another. A man was seated on his motorcycle; a young person was in a big chair with his Gameboy in his hands (https://abcnews.go.com/US/dead-people-life-poses-funerals/story?id=23456853). These ideas do not reflect a Catholic or even a Christian mindset of death.

Some of the suggestions offered in this chapter will not be easy for family members to hear. You must pray about the right words to say, and if harsh words are spoken in the ensuing conversation with the family, pray that you may let them roll off you, so that you will be able to serve the family. Some days in ministry are just more difficult than others.

CHAPTER FOUR

Meeting the Family

Earlier, I wrote about preplanning funerals, but in reality there will be a small percentage of your parishioners who have done this. Most likely, you will be meeting with family members a couple of days before the funeral to make all the arrangements. Who leads these meetings in your parish? The priest? Music or liturgy director? Pastoral care person? Or a bereavement minister? In truth, it can be any one or combination of these ministers, though it often makes things easier if the priest and music person are the primary people involved. It helps the priest to be a part of the Scripture choices and to hear family stories and things for the homily or to know more about the loved one. As was evidenced earlier in walking through the funeral rite, it is ultimately his responsibility to choose the Scriptures. Or he may choose to delegate that responsibility to one of the ministers mentioned above.

Involving the primary parish musician makes it a lot easier especially when people have obscure music requests, or when a family member may be involved in the service. Being part of the planning can save a lot of calls and emails later.

Though these sessions are sometimes challenging, this is one of the most sacred journeys you may walk with someone, and it is an honor to be there. When family members arrive, you will likely put every psychological and spiritual and interpersonal relationship skill you have to the test. No two sessions are alike, and you need to be prepared for just about anything to happen. Perhaps they are active parishioners you can share a hug with and feel the loss of the deceased, but more often you are meeting with strangers. You can quickly determine which siblings do not get along, or who hasn't spoken to their dad in years. It is also painfully obvious within a couple of minutes which members are still practicing their Catholic faith, which relative is the fundamentalist, and which kids are agnostic. All of these situations are like potential land mines waiting to explode. It is your job to navigate them through this hour or so, and help them leave with a sense of hope, knowing that they have helped plan a beautiful resurrection service.

Sometimes families are very quiet, or sad, or just plain lost. They may need to be guided through every step of the process. In other families, people are joking and laughing, and they jump right into the planning. It's important to know when you can step back and let them find their way through the Scriptures and music. It is a delicate balance. In many situations, there is at least one dominant sibling, and another who is very introverted or passive. In those situations it is very important to make sure that the quiet one gets their voice heard.

Start each session with a prayer, and go around the table to get the names of the people present. If you are not good at remembering, quickly write them down for reference throughout the week. When the person who has died is not well known to you, it might be good to start actual planning by listening to family members tell of their passing, or to ask simple questions like "Tell me about your dad?" or "What is one word you would use to describe your mom?" or "What is a favorite memory of your brother? What was his faith like?" Usually a simple question like that is like a little bit of leaven and will start the conversation rolling. If you have a chance to print off the obituary in advance, that may give you an idea as well, but sometimes people simply repeat it. Look for answers with a bit more depth, and they may help you plan the liturgy. Often while this is taking place, the notes you jot down can help you think of Scripture passages and music choices that are most fitting.

We already spoke of the organization of a good planning guide in the chapter on preplanning funerals. Have multiple copies available so that everyone can see. Print them in a font large enough to be easily read. Don't rush the process. Guide them through the proceedings slowly, focusing on one reading at a time to literally keep people on the same page, lest you have one person talking about the Old Testament while another has already gone on to Gospel readings. You may need to prime the pump by suggesting a reading or two, or they may jump in with both feet. You'll quickly sense how they will operate best.

When a family member has found a reading they like, invite everybody to take a look at it. Perhaps this will spur other suggestions. Make sure that there is some sort of a general consensus before going on to the next reading. Sometimes families may let each person pick a reading, or sometimes they may leave it to the one most active in church, but try and engage them all as best as you can, and make sure all voices are heard. Again, be mindful of that quiet introvert in the bunch.

As mentioned, when planning the music, it is very helpful to have the music director there. In my experience, when I am not present, the liturgy is much more likely to fall back to those cookie-cutter choices. The music director's presence will be helpful, and being part of the process will also help the director pray more at the funeral itself.

People may not know the songs by title, especially the responsorial psalms, but singing a bit of them can help them know what they like and dislike. A knowledge of hymns is certainly helpful, especially if they want something that is off the beaten path. This has also been helpful when someone has requested something obscure for the prelude. Similarly, one may request a certain classical piece, but the musician can tell you if they are capable of pulling it off with a day's notice before the funeral. Sometimes there are family members who wish to be involved musically.

THE FUNERAL MASS— EULOGY OR REMARKS OF REMEMBRANCE?

Sometimes when planning, the first thing a family will tell you is that certain persons are "doing the eulogies." By definition a eulogy is a "speech or piece of writing that praises someone or something highly, typically someone who has just died." As stated earlier, there is no place for a eulogy in a Catholic Funeral Mass.

As the rite guides us:

> A brief homily based on the readings should always be given at the funeral liturgy, but never any kind of eulogy. The homilist should dwell on God's compassionate love and on the paschal mystery of the Lord as proclaimed in the Scripture readings. Through the homily, the community should receive the consolation and strength to face the death of one of its members with a hope that has been nourished by the proclamation of the saving word of God. ▪ **OCF 141**

The rite does say that "a member or a friend of the family may speak in remembrance of the deceased before the final commendation begins" (170). While this allows for someone to make remarks, it is very problematic at that point. Realistically, it disturbs the beauty and the flow of the liturgy, and appears to be an acceptance of reality, e.g., "Well, we have to let them speak some place." Often the person giving remarks will have spent the whole liturgy worrying about the points they are going to share. Similarly, people are "ready to be done" with the funeral by this point, and do not listen well. Because of this, many parishes that allow remarks of remembrance have moved them to before the liturgy begins.

It is important to have your policy on this written clearly, or during emotional times family members will insist on much more. For example, your policy might be "one speaker for three to five minutes" or "two pages typed." It is important that you do not encourage a speaker to just "wing it," because these remarks can go on for very long or become a second homily. This is often the case if relatives practice another religion, because they may want to get their particular brand of salvation in, or say everything they think the priest is going to miss about their loved one.

The reality is, no one can ever tell all there is to say about someone in a few brief remarks, so helping them be succinct is the best thing you can do. If someone insists they need fifteen minutes to speak about their loved one, or two people want to share, then some parishes shut down the visitation early, or list it in the obituary as "Remarks of Remembrance at 1:45 PM, Funeral Mass at 2:00 PM." This may also be the case if someone wants an extended musical prelude, or to show a long video to those gathered ahead of time.

Listing this correctly in the obituary and funeral notice saves those who may be late arrivals the disappointment of not being able to see the casket or greet the family. It is only fair to those involved in ministry at the funeral to start at the time listed. For example, if the funeral is supposed to start at 2:00 PM, and twenty minutes of remarks start then, it likely means you won't be done with the funeral until 3:30, and that may pose difficulties for a cantor, musician, servers taken from school, or members of a bereavement team who planned on being there a certain length of time.

It is also very important for the funeral home and church to be in sync on this topic. That way, they can publish the correct information in the obituary, and they know what time to start moving things and shutting down the line during visitation. The better working relationship you can have with the funeral home, the smoother everything will go.

TECHNOLOGY AND THE LITURGY

Similarly, you may want to have a policy in place regarding any audiovisual elements of the prelude or the liturgy. For example, if your parish has screens or TVs in the narthex and the family wishes to show a presentation during the visitation, let them know what format you prefer and have them bring it in ahead of time to troubleshoot. For example, "Presentations must be in MP4 format on a thumb drive," or "Send files to [this address] in Dropbox, so they may be loaded to the parish computer in advance," or "There is an HDMI cable available. To avoid difficulties in translation, please bring your device (phone, tablet, computer) with the presentation on it." Never take it for granted that things will work. With technology changing so rapidly, there are many platforms available, and they don't all play nicely with each other. I have had some pretty nervous moments trying to troubleshoot tech issues when people handed me a disk five minutes before a visitation started and it was not in a format that our system recognized.

As in the case of remarks of remembrance, it is also important to think about what sorts of pictures are included. Are the stories and pictures of happy hour a good idea? How will blue language be avoided? Sometimes what should be obvious to people is not, and people can make very inappropriate choices. It never hurts to remind people that some things are best left for the reception afterward, or in the privacy of the family home rather than over the microphone or screens.

WHO IS INVOLVED IN LITURGICAL MINISTRIES AT THE FUNERAL?

As we have noted, many times family members are not practicing Catholics. This can cause some snafus when it comes to liturgical ministries. Let's take a walk through the various ministries involved.

Placing the Pall

At the beginning of the rite, there is the placing of the funeral pall. This is a simple, loving gesture, like draping one in the baptismal garment. Remind folks they do not have to say anything, so it doesn't matter how emotional they are; they can do this. The funeral home can do this if no one in the family wants to, but it is surely more meaningful if family members do it. I have explained to the adult children of the deceased, "think of all the times your mom tucked you in—wrapping her in the pall is one last chance to tuck *her* in." Similarly, the laying on of Christian symbols can be done by anybody. But if mom didn't pray the Rosary, why are you burying her with one? Or putting it on the coffin? Don't just do it because it is the "Catholic" thing to do.

Sacred Scripture

Who should proclaim the Scripture readings is a touchy subject. Some families want to be involved, and some want nothing to do with it; but in any case the reader should be someone who can proclaim the readings without falling apart. We have all been at a funeral that was absolutely painful as a family member sniffed her way through the readings, or read so fast and soft that no one could hear it. If family members are going to read, give them a copy of the Scriptures to prepare in advance. The day of the funeral, take them up ahead of time and show them the microphone and ambo so that they may be comfortable. Let them practice through the PA system. The reader does not have to be a practicing Catholic, but should be someone who can proclaim the word.

Offertory Presentation of the Gifts

When we think of taking up the gifts, it would seem to make sense to entrust this to those who could receive the Body and Blood of Christ, but many times the family wants this done by grandchildren or other members who may be nonpracticing.

The only things brought forward in the presentation are the wine and the hosts. This is not the place to bring forth a rose from each grandchild, or grandma or grandpa's poker chips, or a mini John Deere tractor. Those are things for the visitation, or post-committal at the graveside or at the reception. It is important to hear that I'm not saying there is anything wrong with these types of gestures; they simply don't belong in the Catholic funeral liturgy. If a family wants to have everyone take a flower from the casket spray at the committal, or set off balloons, or have grandpa's toy trains displayed in the narthex, that is fine. As the *General Instruction of the Roman Missal* reminds us, all that should be brought up in the procession are the "bread and wine for the celebration of the Eucharist or of other gifts to relieve the needs of the Church and of the poor" (140).

Extraordinary Ministers of Communion

Extraordinary Ministers always need to be practicing Catholics. Ideally, they should be people who are trained ahead of time and serve in this ministry regularly. Every parish has slightly different procedures so be sure to walk people through things ahead of time.

Musicians

Working with guest musicians can be a potential pitfall at a funeral, and it is a time to put on your best pastoral self. Oftentimes, people want to bring in a family friend or relative to be part of the liturgy. Before you determine how they will be involved, it is good to get a sense of their background. Are they Catholic? Are they familiar with cantoring a Catholic liturgy? Do they play an instrument? Will they need a power source, mic, or other electric equipment? How old are they (e.g., child or adult)?

When you have this information, it is easier for you to discern with the family how the musical guests will be involved. Perhaps you may want to suggest they do their pieces as a prelude, e.g., if it is a grandchild playing a piano piece, or a friend of the family who wrote a song and will be accompanying himself on guitar. Or maybe there is room for a solo piece as a thanksgiving at Communion. Similarly, there is a huge difference between a fine pianist or organist and someone who knows the Catholic Funeral Rite. A parish musician must be used.

In rare cases, someone is a trained cantor in their home parish, and it will be fine to have them do the whole liturgy. But be cautious: there are so many Mass settings available these days, and multiple Catholic publishers, so you may not have the same repertoire at all!

One of my most challenging funerals was that of a young person where the family had a friend who was a liturgist in another parish, and they wanted to involve them. Rather than all of us meeting together, the family went to plan the funeral with that person first, leaving the priest and me to pick up the pieces at our parish. While we gave this person clear and concise instructions on the way things were done in our parish, this liturgist ignored them, and it left me in the very difficult position of having to tell the family, "No, you cannot do that," and finding ways to compromise and to "play nice" with this other musician.

Whatever your situation, think carefully about how you phrase any responses with the family. These are delicate times, and you may not want them to know or see what is really going through your mind at that moment. That being said, as much as there is a need to be pastoral, it is important to remember that just because someone may want something, it may not always be appropriate. You have to be the one to keep that delicate balance and say "no" when necessary. Finding a positive way to spin it, such as throwing out another option, or empathizing with disappointment, may get you further than explaining a bunch of rubrics to someone.

When planning the funeral is complete, it is often helpful to take the family to the parish and show them the space, explaining things like, "Here is where the casket will be during the visitation," "This is what our ossuary looks like," "When it is time to place the pall you will be standing here," "Don't worry if you forget when to go up to read. Father will provide you with gentle clues." Explain to them that their loved one will be remembered in weekend Masses offered in the parish, and that the whole parish family is praying for them.

So, we have talked about planning a funeral, and what it may entail. Let us continue to discuss how the parish family may be involved in this celebration.

CHAPTER FIVE

The Parish Family and the Funeral *Funeral Ministers*

SOMETIMES, WHEN FAMILIES COME INTO THE CHURCH FOR A VISITATION AND FUNERAL, it may seem like they are simply people renting the parish for a few hours; there is a huge disconnect between them and the actual parish. But this is not the way things should be. We must remember that "burying the dead" is one of the Corporal Works of Mercy and should, therefore, be a parish event. Parishes choose to handle this in many different ways. Let us look at a few simple examples.

The parish staff is clearly involved in the funeral in any number of ways, from the administrative assistant who takes the first call from the family, to the janitor who sets up tables and chairs for the reception or makes sure the bathrooms are clean. Does your parish have a clear flow chart and check-off sheet to make sure that no pieces are being left undone? Emails about funerals go out to more than a dozen people in my parish. Clear communication will save a world of headaches. (Examples of items to consider in a flow chart may be found at Appendix V.)

In many situations, it makes sense to use parish lectors and Extraordinary Ministers of Communion at a funeral. These people know the drill. They are used to reading and are familiar with the mic system at the parish. They know where the EMs stand, and what to do with the sacred vessels afterward. They remember to give communion to the music ministers and the choir. (At my parish through the years, there have been several priests and multiple EMs at funerals who forgot to give communion to the choir, even though we are located right by the sanctuary.) In parishes where an EM must go to the choir loft it is even more important to have someone familiar with the task. Besides those practical, logistical aspects, because they are not as emotionally involved with the funeral, a parish lector may be able to proclaim the word better.

There are many times in the course of a liturgy where priest, cantor, and musician may be connecting by simple eye movement or facial expression. Knowing and recognizing each other's signals is key to it all running smoothly. There are times when people want a very simple, quiet service, and I have been known to respect that and both play and cantor. Other times, people are asking for just a solo cantor. A beautiful voice adds so much to the liturgy, but it should never be about being a soloist. The cantor is the psalmist and is to lead the congregation in musical prayer.

In most cases, people will follow the lead you offer them. If you ask, "Do you want a cantor or the choir?" they may think it is more expensive or a bother, or something else. Generally I suggest that we will have a cantor and a choir, and explain that this is the ministry of the volunteer choir.

By using a parish cantor and/or a resurrection choir, you are providing musicians familiar with the hymns, psalms, and Mass parts, as well as any idiosyncrasies of the given priests and parish. Not only do they provide a rich musical canvas for the liturgy, there are people who can respond to the priest during the dialogue portions of the liturgy. This is especially helpful when many attending the funeral are not practicing Catholics.

The Second Letter to the Corinthians 5:20 speaks of being "ambassadors for Christ…." I use this with my resurrection choir, explaining they are "ambassadors for Christ, and for the parish." I also remind them of the Corporal Works of Mercy. This is something they "get" very intuitively, and people are totally devoted to this ministry. Because some of our folks are senior citizens who are still not internet savvy, we work with a calling tree and typically ask people to be there thirty to forty minutes before a funeral, or earlier if there is difficult music or something special. If they can be there, great! And if not, well, God always seems to give us the perfect group that we need.

I recall that when we first began this ministry someone in the parish thought it was something special just for "the important people," and they made a snide comment. I said, "Yes, that is right, it is for everybody." Near that time, the choir came together to sing for two funerals the same week. One was for a man well known in the parish, with three hundred people in attendance. It was a lovely, rich liturgy. The other was for a old lady and there were only about a dozen in attendance, many nonpracticing. There were as many present in the choir as in the congregation. The choir added a dignity and elegance to the liturgy. Afterwards, a savvy old gentleman from the choir came up to me and said, "You know, it was really nice that we were at Bill's funeral on Tuesday." And he paused a moment, "But it was really necessary that we were at Martha's today."

It is hard to get new people to commit to our regular church choir, especially young people. But it seems there are frequently new people joining the resurrection choir. Often what happens is that someone is at a funeral, and they are touched by the presence of the choir and then choose to become a member of it. Some parishes may have stricter guidelines, but in my parish it is a very fluid ministry.

Altar servers may be students or adults. Some parish schools allow students out of class to serve a funeral, but kids are so busy these days it may be hard to get servers for Saturdays. Consider training some adults for this ministry. Besides having more flexible schedules, these persons could also take on the role of sacristan, setting up before the liturgy and cleaning up afterward. This may be especially helpful when Father has to go to the cemetery right after the funeral or is balancing a very heavy schedule.

Some parishes have actual bereavement ministries with many varying tasks. In some cases, there are volunteers trained to plan the liturgy and work closely alongside the priest and musician. In other instances this is more a ministry of hospitality. They may greet family and guests at the visitation, set out water and tissues, point out restrooms, hand out orders of worship, serve as ushers during communion, be altar servers, sacristans, or assist Father in any other ways. They may run audiovisual equipment or record the funeral for families. Occasionally members of this team may create the order of worship. Some assist with funeral luncheons as well.

In some cases, these people also do follow-up ministry with the family and are a big part of the November Mass of Remembrance. If you do not have a formal bereavement ministry, I urge you to consider establishing one. As ministers and staff are increasingly spread thinner and thinner across a wider array of jobs, these volunteer ministries become more and more important.

With the increase in cremations and the high cost of funerals we have noticed another trend in recent years. As people try and cut corners on expenses, they do not realize what the funeral home staff actually does at a funeral, so they will say, "Oh we didn't have them come. We are doing it ourselves." Then they will proceed to ask, "Um, is there a table that we can set our pictures on?" "Do you have easels we can borrow for picture boards?" and all the things the home usually does.

They don't know to take pictures or record who the floral arrangements are from, or which ones may need to be removed from the sanctuary before the liturgy starts. Similarly, there is no one to gently move the visitation line along when the end of the allotted time is drawing near, and no one to line the family up to enter into the church. There are a hundred details that are taken for granted that all of the sudden end up in the priest's or liturgist's lap. The priest may be coming in from another meeting and event and not have time for these, or be overwhelmed with these details while he is trying to prepare himself spiritually for the Mass. By having a bereavement team in place, or to call on, you could avoid this type of situation. In any event, come up with a list of things a family may want to remember when they take on the funeral themselves.

Even if you do not have a specific ministry like this, it might be time to contact the head of your ushers and see if you could pick up a few volunteers for the day, or ask the sacristan from morning Mass if he could set up for the funeral liturgy. Similarly, have a list of a few folks who are willing to serve as lectors or Extraordinary Ministers of Communion. That way you are not trying to be many places at once, and it will assure the funeral begins in a dignified, solemn manner rather than in a frenzied rush.

Remember: you are getting a chance to minister to a lot of people who may not have been in your church or any church in a while. The experience you provide them may shape their future return or response. You have a chance to evangelize in an important way here. Not by an altar call or a fire and brimstone homily, but through the example of loving hospitality and welcome.

Sometimes, as ministers working for the church, we can get busy with our role and not see what others do. Perhaps it is time to get a small focus group of trusted individuals or ask your prayer and worship committee or stewardship committee to talk about these issues. The beautiful thing is, there is no one-size-fits-all bereavement package. Your bereavement ministry does not have to look like any other parish's program. You might want to find out what is being done at neighboring parishes. Take a look at your weaknesses and areas where you are struggling, or areas where you are doing well but could always improve. Create your ministry to focus on these needs. However the ministries are organized in your parish, try to provide a seamless garment from planning, to funeral, to bereavement, to Mass of Remembrance. The successful minister relies on volunteers and knows how to delegate well.

CHAPTER SIX

O Death! How Bitter Is the Thought

Dealing with Difficult Funerals

> O death! How bitter is the thought of you
> for the one at peace in his home,
> For the one who is serene and always successful,
> who can still enjoy life's pleasures.
>
> **SIRACH 41:1**

MOST OF THE TIME, ONCE A FUNERAL IS PLANNED AND THE MINISTRIES ARE ASSIGNED, THINGS PROCEED FAIRLY UNEVENTFULLY. Parishes have many funerals, and though the readings and music may change, the rite is the same each time. There is peace and comfort in that. That is the beauty and power of ritual. Yet there are the other funerals that are incredibly difficult for the families, for staff, and for all those involved.

These are the painful stories, like the death of a child, a young person killed in a car accident, or someone in the prime of their life being taken down by cancer. These stories can be very stressful and involve a lot of extra work, so it is always important to remember self care during these days. Make sure you are praying, eating right, and getting out for a walk to clear your head from time to time. Perhaps you as a parish staff will pray together. Besides families being emotionally distraught and spiritually numb, you need to be prepared for the large number of people who will come out for this visitation and funeral, and for any number of complications that arise.

In these cases of tragedy, sometimes waiting three days for a funeral is too long for the local community. They need a place for their grief right now. Consider celebrating an evening prayer service, or the Office of the Dead. We did this in the case of a young college student who died a violent death, and of a high school athlete who died in a car accident. The experiences were extremely different, but both were profound. For the college student, there were readings and hymns, and it was an initial chance for the priest to speak on that difficult "Why did this happen?" question. It allowed people to deal with their initial grief. The family was not interacting with people that night, so nothing was held back, and people sobbed freely.

In the case of the high schooler, hundreds of students showed up, along with a number of teachers and coaches. Many members of the parish staff were also there with lanyards to identify them. There was a simple reading, and the priest literally sat down in a chair in the sanctuary and just had a heart to heart with the kids. Then they were invited to talk to each other. The church provided a space for these kids to hug and cry and talk and comfort each other for the next two hours.

In situations like this, you are dealing with a short period of time and may not have energy to be creative. Before you reinvent the wheel, look at the ritual that is available to you and then consider how you may want to adapt it for your particular needs and situation. You may end up utilizing the Office for the Dead, or the Prayers for the Dead and Mourners, or pieces from the Funerals for Children to help you out. Start with the rites and the prayers and adapt from there. In these high profile cases, you may be dealing with different items besides the normal funeral pieces.

HIGH PROFILE FUNERALS

In one extremely high profile case, the priest, pastoral associate, and I went to meet with the family at the funeral home. This was not to plan the readings and music for the liturgy, but just to figure out all the other aspects of how we were all going to make it through the week. This was going to be a big news story, and the TV channels were already all over the family.

It was determined that any press releases would come through the parish website. The priest would be the spokesperson for the family, and one of the staff would be the communications contact person with media. It was winter and thirty degrees below outside that week, so we also determined with the funeral home the best plan of action to utilize the church and narthex during the visitation so people would not be waiting outside. The family also made it very clear that they did not want the media present during the funeral itself.

We knew that the media had a task to do too, and they would be diligent until they got the job done, so we decided to work with them as best we could. There was an Evening Prayer service the first day after the death, and they were allowed to film from the back of the church so that no family faces would be shown but so they had some live footage. Then, we allowed them to come into the church when it was empty to film some "B roll" footage of the vigil lights, crucifix, and sanctuary, etc., that they could combine with outdoor shots for the story itself the day of the funeral.

We fed them with regular media updates, and allowed them access to the parish Wi-fi. Because it was so cold, the day of the funeral we allowed them to take over the parish conference room as a communications center instead of having to film outside, and we kept a pot of coffee, water, and donuts handy. Afterward, they commented that they had never been treated so well. In a period of time when the Catholic Church often has a black eye in the press, they were pleasantly surprised, and it afforded the family the privacy that they deserved while allowing the news to do its jobs. Dignity was maintained.

Another simple piece of advice is this: the community will want to help. Let them. Walmart provided cases of water for the reception afterward. We had two busloads of college students coming in from out of state for the funeral. Local pizza places delivered pizza for them. Many people who were not even parishioners called and said, "What can we do? What can we bring?" It all worked to create an overwhelming sense of goodness against the evil of this senseless, violent murder.

MILITARY FUNERALS

When dealing with the funeral for an active duty military person, the family is assigned a casualty officer. This person notifies the family of the death of a loved one, and is literally present until after the funeral. They handle all the military pieces and are pretty well versed in ritual. You will need to work with them in all aspects of planning and will end up with a very strict timeline for the day of the funeral itself. For example, "At exactly 16:45, soldiers will remove the American flag from the casket and fold it, and present it to the mother of the deceased."

Be prepared for both the positive and negative aspects of a military funeral as well. Perhaps hundreds of Vietnam-era biker veterans may be there with American flags and will want to flank the church through the entire visitation. If you had water and sandwiches for them it would be a nice gesture of hospitality. Sadly, you might also have a crazy fundamentalist protest group to deal with too. One can only hope their protest permit limits them to a spot a block away.

Any of these large celebrations may also mean that you may have additional church and government officials present. Be prepared to let these VIPs have a place to visit with the family in private, or to cut through the receiving line. The funeral home will surely bring a large staff to any of these large services.

We have already talked about bereavement teams, but parish staff presence is also extremely important at times like these. It is very helpful to have staff and volunteers wearing nametags or visible lanyards so guests may find the assistance they need.

It is one of those "and extra duties as assigned" kind of days. You might be looking for a rope or something to make another wrap around in the receiving line, checking the toilet paper in the bathroom, printing off another hundred copies of the order of worship, or you might simply be focusing on the ministry of being present. By listening to others and their grief, you may take some of the pressure off of the family. Similarly, people will simply remember seeing that the staff was present.

THE DEATH OF A YOUNG CHILD

Perhaps the hardest funerals of all are of young children. Maybe an infant is stillborn or only lives a few hours, or a child may die of crib death, or a young child may have fought a valiant battle with a terminal illness until their little body had nothing left to fight with. In these instances, the family will likely be devastated. They will need much gentle, loving care, and careful guidance in the planning.

In situations like this, even though the funeral rite has a special section of readings for the death of a child, the last thing I want to do is hand someone a book with multiple options and say, "Choose." In the Scripture readings the rite provides for Death of a Baptized Child and Death of an Unbaptized Child, the rite teaches us something important if we are reading between the lines. There are very few "official" Scripture choices given, and in all instances they are briefer than the readings for an adult funeral. In some cases, the reading from Isaiah or Lamentations or Romans is the same basic reading from the adult lectionary, but it has been pared down and simplified for the children's portion.

Study the rite and you will find: "The minister, in consultation with those concerned, chooses those rites that best correspond to the particular needs and customs of the mourners. In some instances, for example, the death of an infant, only the rite of committal and perhaps one of the forms of prayer with the family may be desirable" (OCF 235).

Similarly, it reminds us, "Those involved in planning the funeral rites for a deceased child should take into account the age of the child, the circumstances of death, the grief of the family, and the needs and customs of those taking part in the rites" (OCF 243).

I believe this speaks volumes for the need to keep things very simple. No one wants some heady theological Scripture text that is hard to understand. What they need is a simple phrase or image that they may grasp hold of to find some strength and faith during this difficult time. Do some careful preplanning yourself before you meet with the family. Select a few readings in advance that may be apt for the situation, and gently offer them. The family will surely be grateful for your guidance. Similarly, prepare music suggestions in advance as well.

Sometimes, in situations like this, music selections may also be out of the box from the normal "Catholic hymns," e.g., perhaps the child sang "Jesus Loves Me," or something else that will offer the family comfort.

I can recall the funeral of a person with special needs. Their favorite song was "Silent Night," so at the preparation of the gifts in the middle of July we sang "Sleep in heavenly peace." We are all familiar with the old joke, "What is the difference between a liturgist and a terrorist?" but while it is important to make sure the rites are being observed correctly, it is also so very important to be pastoral, especially at times like this.

The OCF makes two other points very clearly. In number 240, it reminds that there may be ministers in the community who can help the family better at times like this, e.g., someone who has been through it. It never hurts to ask oneself, "Am I the best person for the job?" If the answer is "no," enlist the help of others. Perhaps it is not just spiritual ministry we are talking about. With social media tools it is easy to use something like "Signup Genius," "Meal Train," or "Take Them a Meal." One can help a family through a tough time. This would be another good task for a bereavement ministry, not just in that first week of grief but for a while until some semblance of normalcy returns. While we are speaking of the death of a child, this kind of bereavement ministry wold also be of immense help to the newly widowed or those in many other situations. After my mother passed away, my dad jokingly said, "I've made lots of new friends. Mrs. Campbell, Mrs. Dinty Moore, Mrs. Paul's," as he was thrust into the world of cooking for himself.

The last point is to get the family involved, and adapt the rite as necessary to do so.

> Special consideration should be given to any sisters, brothers, friends or classmates of the deceased child who may be present at the funeral rites. Children will be better able to take part in the celebration if the various elements are planned

and selected with them in mind: texts, readings, music, gesture, processions, silence. The minister may wish to offer brief remarks for the children's benefit at suitable points during the celebration. [*Author's note:* With the number of non-Catholics at many funerals this is not a bad idea anyway!]

If children will be present at the funeral rites, those with requisite ability should be asked to exercise some of the liturgical roles. During the funeral Mass, for example, children may serve as readers, acolytes, or musicians, or assist in the readings of the general intercessions and in the procession with the gifts. Depending upon the age and numbers of children taking part, adaptations recommended in the *Directory for Masses with Children* may be appropriate. ▪ **OCF 242**

FUNERALS WITH A BISHOP

There are times when you may be celebrating a funeral Mass with a bishop present. It might be the death of a priest or deacon, the death of a priest's parent, a public situation, or just someone that the bishop knows well. If you are not familiar with the procedures, you may want to check in with your diocesan worship office.

In the case of a priest's parent, the priest would be the one to celebrate the Mass. The bishop would be there in choir vestments, and he would not concelebrate. (*Note:* If the bishop were in Mass vestments he, as the highest ranking cleric, would need to be the main celebrant. However, if a bishop is present at another bishop's mother's funeral, he would vest.) If the bishop is to give the Final Commendation he would usually replace the choir dress with cope, stole, and mitre so that he may direct the prayers.

For the funeral of a priest or deacon, the bishop would usually celebrate. You would need to make sure that the funeral rite and orders of worship are approved by the worship office. In fact, the office may produce the worship aids, or take the lead with the funeral, and provide you with the necessary information. All priests must have their funeral plan on file at the chancery office.

In any of these instances, be mindful that there will likely be concelebrants. Make sure there is a separate space for the bishop to vest, and space for the concelebrants. Be mindful to reserve pews for the concelebrants if they will not be in the sanctuary. Is the bishop's emcee coming? Are additional servers needed? There are many more details that must be thought through and carefully planned. Do not be afraid to ask for assistance from your diocesan worship office.

SELF CARE

There is an old adage that death comes in threes. So, sometimes, do challenging situations. In one of the most difficult weeks of my ministry, we had three funerals in the days right before Christmas, and in between Christmas and New Year's we had funerals for a child, a Marine, and a priest. While I was ministering to the families, I was almost reaching overload myself. During times like this, it is important to make sure that you are eating, praying, exercising, and resting.

It is also important to ask for help when you need it. For example, as liturgist and music director, I direct while accompanying at fifty to sixty funerals a year. But when it is going to be a "biggie" I often bring in another accompanist. This allows me to be "liturgist" and move back and forth, taking care of any last-minute communications with the presider or the funeral home before the service starts. This also allows me to step in at the last second when a cantor is too emotionally distraught to sing, and allows me to be on high alert for the other things that could happen that I may miss while behind the keyboard. Similarly, I may have been so busy with other details preparing for the funeral along with my regular weekly work tasks that there was no practice time. Knowing when to delegate is a good thing; it is a sign of strength.

If a pastor has an influx of funerals, it means multiple homilies to prepare and the challenges of "being present" to the families and finding the sheer energy all this takes. Look at your schedule and ask, "What has to be here?" Don't be afraid to cancel that council meeting, or appointment, or find a sub to take one of your daily Masses. Schedule the deacons or bereavement ministers to do the Vigil or to go to the cemetery. Find time for your silence. Continue to go to the well of prayer to be refreshed. Remember that you can't give away something you haven't got. These are not the occasions for canned homilies and bad platitudes. We need to always give our very best self in whatever ministry we serve. Everyone is owed that dignity, but the family will also remember these events and how you handled them. This can also factor in directly to the next time you see this family in church.

CHAPTER SEVEN

O Death! How Welcome Is Your Sentence to the Weak

Funerals for the Elderly

> O death! How welcome is your sentence
> to the weak, failing in strength,
> Stumbling and tripping on everything,
> with sight gone and hope lost.
>
> ■ SIRACH 41:2

WHILE WE HAVE SPOKEN ABOUT DIFFICULT FUNERALS, THERE ARE SURELY TIMES WHEN DEATH IS A RELIEF. Perhaps the person has had an extended illness, been confined to a care center with Alzheimer's, or been grieving a lost spouse. Or maybe one has simply lived a good long life and it is time to go home to God.

These provide another type of challenge to a parish staff. It can be easy to be complacent or let the funeral be just one more thing to check off in a busy week. But remember that while this may be very familiar for us, death is still new or unfamiliar for the family. While someone may smile and say, "Yes, Mom lived a good life," and be fine with the funeral, grandchildren may be experiencing death for the first time, or the deceased person may be very beloved.

One must be just as empathetic and present to the family in a situation like this as in any difficult circumstances. One must recognize that each unique family also grieves differently. It is easy to do a mental eye roll when someone is sobbing during the funeral of an eighty-year-old. But they may be grieving that they never healed a relationship, or there could be any number of factors that we are not aware of. At a recent funeral for a ninety-seven-year-old, the level of grief the family expressed was as much as if their loved one had been in the prime of their life. They simply loved the person so much it still seemed like death was "too soon." Be present and gentle in any situation, without being condescending.

Another scenario is that someone may have almost no family left, and they might be planning a distant relative's funeral. These are the moments when we really need to step up our game and be present, rather than thinking, "Ho hum, 'the souls of the just are in the hands of God....' I got this."

And while we have talked about how important bereavement ministry and resurrection choirs are, it may be at these very small funerals where we are really doing the Corporal Works of Mercy. Whatever you do, be present. Don't phone in your ministry!

There may be times when you are called to plan a funeral for someone who has no family, or may be a pauper, or little is known about them. You will still want to do a service that pays dignity to the deceased. Find parish ministers to serve as lectors and servers. Announce it at a Sunday liturgy, or ask your daily Mass crowd if they can attend.

I am always mindful of the example that an old parishioner set for me. Eddie went to every funeral there was at our church. I asked him once, "Wow, do you really know all these people?" and while he had been a lifelong resident of the town and actually knew many of them, he said once, "No, I don't, but I have the time, and I am here to pray for them."

Similarly, a pastor would start nearly every homily by reminding those gathered that that was our purpose. We were gathered there to pray for the repose of the soul of the departed, and that wasn't something people took much time to do these days. He always thanked the people for being there and let them know how important their ministry of presence and praying was.

It is just as essential for us to give one hundred ten percent at any funeral we are a part of. The lights and air need to be on for twelve people as well as one hundred. The same sort of hospitality must be provided for all. Please don't take things for granted.

CHAPTER EIGHT

Ethnic and Cultural Adaptations

ONE MAY FIND THAT WHILE THE *ORDER OF CHRISTIAN FUNERALS* IS USED THROUGHOUT THE COUNTRY, there are some differences in the way the funeral is celebrated in different geographic regions, as well as in different ethnic and cultural situations. Some of these may be as simple as a beloved hymn, and others may be full blown instances of liturgical inculturation. Let us look at a few of those examples.

NATIVE AMERICAN FUNERALS

Many times, Native American funerals and celebrations of death are a combination of Catholic and Native American spiritualities. Traditions may vary greatly between tribes, but hospitality is critically important to all. Feeding the guests is a very important piece of the culture. The wake itself usually becomes a multiple-day affair, and in rural regions the priest is present through much of this. Throughout this visitation period, there are often many speakers. While a priest or deacon may speak about the church, members of the tribe will also speak about the traditions and the history of the family, or of the history of someone's name. Many individuals may offer their testimonies, and often area ministers from other churches may speak too. These funerals are the very opposite of the "one and done" funerals; as one liturgist friend described it, "there is story telling for hours, if not days!"

The coffin is sometimes draped with a star quilt instead of a funeral pall. The priest's vestments are often done in a native style, with a quilled or beaded stole, and sacred vessels may also have a Native American theme. Similarly, there may be a Native American corpus on the crucifix. In some cases the use of sage or tobacco "smudging" may replace or be used along with traditional incense. It is a symbol of purification. (*Note:* Sweetgrass, the most common Native American smudging medium, is not typically used at funerals.) There is often a prayer to the four directions, as Native spirituality is very earth-centered. There may also be a sacred pipe involved, or a blessing with an eagle feather. Corporals and purificators may be red. Music may include native hymns and sacred drumming. One may also see things like a coffin being taken to the wake or cemetery in a wagon, or with a riderless horse leading the procession, symbolizing the deceased.

Even movement is important. For example, the guide for Native American liturgy in the Rapid City, South Dakota diocese, "Recommendations for the Inculturation of Lakota Catholicism" (http://www.rapidcitydiocese.org/wp-content/uploads/2014/11/1999-Recom-for-Inc-of-Lak-Cathm.pdf), says "A circle may be incorporated into the celebrations of the Liturgy and prayer services in the present structures where and when possible. For the purpose of

Azilya (incensing), water blessings, distributing communion, ministers move in a sunwise direction—clockwise."

At some point after the Catholic funeral, there may likely be prayers or speeches by medicine men. After the funeral, there is another large meal ceremony called a "give away." At this, star quilts, blankets, food items, and gas cards are given to the guests who have attended. In this culture, you learn to bring a shopping bag with you. Sometimes, things like boiled meat are passed around multiple times, and you are insulting people if you do not take it.

One very important thing to understand about the Native American culture is that they have a very relaxed sense of time. If a funeral is scheduled to start at 1 PM, you might be surprised to look out and see an empty church at that time. Over the next couple of hours people will slowly make their way to the space. There are multiple factors involved. Often, these funerals take place in remote, rural areas. One family may be waiting for someone else to pick them up and give them a ride. Sometimes they are finishing up taking care of animals or other chores, or sometimes, they are just plain running that late. They don't see time the same way corporate America does. You are not insulting someone by being late. You simply wait until people are there, and then it is time to start.

As the Diocese handout says,

> In Lakota ritual the focus is not on clock time, the focus is on the activity itself. It is better to think of Lakota ritual time in terms of order—doing things according to priorities. A ceremony takes precedence over all other activities. People sacrifice other activities in order to be present for the ceremony. They place themselves in a proper frame of mind and the ceremony takes as long as it takes to do it correctly. Length of clock time, short or long, is irrelevant. In the same way the Liturgy of the Eucharist begins when the people assemble and lasts as

> long as it takes for the prayer. No other event takes precedence over the Eucharistic celebration. The people's first priority is to be present at the Eucharist with a good heart. ■ 4

This same attitude is why suggesting "three- to five-minute remarks" from one family member is probably not going to work in this culture. The funeral is not going to be a typical hour-long service. But just as they don't mind arriving late, this culture is not checking their watches to see if it is over yet either. They show up for the duration! Again, you will likely not be blocking off an hour for the funeral, but the day, or multiple days. Understanding this at the outset will save you much frustration.

Often, there is a Native custom of "Keeping the Spirit and Releasing the Spirit." A lock of hair is kept for a year after death, and then this hair is burned to symbolize the releasing of the spirit. This is a pre-Christian tradition that attests to their belief in life beyond the grave.

There are also ceremonies called "the Wiping of Tears" to call the mourners back to the community, and "Blessings of the Headstones."

LATINO CULTURES

One of the first things to note is that people in Latino cultures run on a timeline similar to that described for the Native Americans. They will arrive when they do, and the service will start when it starts.

In many traditional Mexican homes, a funeral home is still not used. The family will often wash and prepare the body, and it is not likely to be embalmed. Nor is it likely to be cremated.

The deceased are displayed for three days, during a *velorio* or wake. They believe it takes three days to determine that the person is really dead. There are many pictures displayed, and multiple rites and prayers. The windows and mirrors are covered with curtains, and they pray many Rosaries and sing traditional Mexican folk music. Under the coffin, they put garlic, alcohol, and onions to ward off evil spirits. Holy cards, candles, and statues of the Sacred Heart and Our Lady of Guadalupe are prevalent.

The deceased may be dressed as a saint. Many women are dressed as Mary, while men may be dressed as an angel. The deceased child is called an *angelito* or "little angel," and there may be a fireworks display to honor the dead.

There will be a procession to the church after the wake, and then on to the pantheon or place of burial. Men will carry the deceased all the way while women pray and cry all the way. A cross of ashes will be made and displayed for a nine-day novena.

Many times, people will place small gifts or holy cards or tokens in the casket. It is not uncommon to hear the *mariachis* playing at the wake.

Perhaps the best known Mexican tradition is *Día de los Muertos*, or "The Day of the Dead," which takes place from October 31–November 2. One will note this is the same time as All Hallow's Eve (Halloween) and All Saints Day. All these traditions existed before Christianity but became an important part of Christianity in their renewed forms.

In *Día de los Muertos*, people believe that souls of the deceased return to the family. One will note candles, exquisitely painted skulls, and many pastries as part of the celebration. During these days, people make altars for praying for the souls of their ancestors and to wait their returns. Sometimes blankets and pillows are laid out for the deceased to rest on at their return.

For those who do use a funeral home, there are homes that now deal especially with ethnic traditions. This article, https://thanatosjournal.files.wordpress.com/2016/06/cann_contemporary1.pdf, speaks about the caterers that are used in specific Latino cultures: "some of the key services at the funeral home included catered food from various countries served at the visitations: enchiladas, burritos, tacos, rice and beans (Mexican-American funerals), and empanadas, arepas, and plantains (Colombian visitations)."

The Latino culture frequently memorializes their dead. They will have prayer cards made up and often offer Masses for the deceased. It is also not unusual to go beyond the obituary and put paid memorial ads in the newspaper at different intervals, e.g., six months, or at yearly anniversaries of the deceased. People often get memorial tattoos as well, with the dates of the deceased and sometimes a picture of them.

In Cuban funeral culture, Catholicism is not as prevalent, and many times it is combined with an African tradition called *Santería*, which does not have Christian beliefs but utilizes Christian symbols. This is also similar to the ways Haitian Catholic and voodoo practices are sometimes combined.

AFRICAN AMERICAN INFLUENCES

In his article on African American Catholic liturgy (http://blog.adw.org/2018/01/gift-african-american-catholic-tradition/), Msgr. Charles Pope makes clear several things about African American Catholic worship in general. One that I found fascinating was that of "Expectation"—that people come with an attitude of expecting to be moved, and that there is a profound experience of being moved by God. Services are often very upbeat and joyous, even in times of trial. Music is a driving factor in the liturgy, and it may be coupled with movement, clapping, and stamping. The priest may elicit a "call and response" type homily, and it is often very lengthy. There is also a sense of freedom, as one assumes that music will not be performed exactly as written on the page. Much will be done by ear or freestyle, and there is room for creative expression. One is likely to hear spirituals or gospel hymns. Nor will a funeral take just an hour. Everyone in attendance will be dressed in their best, and it will not be uncommon to see a mixture of very sharp looking suits and dresses and African dashikis. Closely related to the African American funeral is what I would call the New Orleans Style Funeral.

NEW ORLEANS FUNERAL

When I spoke to Betty Ann Hickey from the Office of Worship of the Archdiocese of New Orleans, she explained that the percentage of cremations was much higher in this region. Again, this is a decision driven primarily by economics and sheer reality. All burials in that area are above ground. And unless a family owns an existing mausoleum or burial space, the cost of one is prohibitive to most people; therefore the family goes with cremation.

She also mentioned that Louisiana had pretty loose laws around burial and cremation, so it was not uncommon for folks to rent a casket, or even just use a shroud. So for many cases, the body is present for the Funeral Mass, and the cremation then takes place later on.

Wakes are not as common, and visitations are likely to be before the service begins at the church. Within the liturgy itself, two of the songs you are most likely to hear are "This Little Light of Mine" and "Just a Closer Walk with Thee." The latter is a standard ending song in this region.

It is when the funeral itself is over that things may get interesting. As they move to the cemetery or as the group moves from the church service to the repast (reception), they have what is known as the second line. Even if a funeral is closed to the public, this is open to anyone and is often the time for the community at large to pay respects to the deceased. For example, when the owner of the New Orleans Saints died early this year, this was what the obituary said: "There will be an invitation-only Funeral Mass at the Cathedral. Following the Mass, there will be a public second line through the French Quarter." And the route was listed.

The second line will likely include a horse-drawn carriage with the coffin, family, friends, and clergy walking in line, and a whole marching jazz band. In its most traditional form, the music starts very slowly and solemnly, e.g., a slow version of "Just a Closer Walk With Thee," but as it leaves the cemetery, or moves closer to the place of the repast, it picks up steam with a festive version of "When the Saints" and other such songs. Traditional marching band instruments meld with those of Zydeco to create these unusual experiences.

Betty Ann Hickey also told me that while these second-line traditions are much beloved, what is often lost is the theology that used to accompany them. Many of the people on the street may just be thinking "party." The realization that the solemn tone is celebrating the death, and the joyful party is once more an expression of our hope in the resurrection, is often lost. In recent funerals there is less likely to be a distinction between the solemn and joyful music times.

EUROPEAN FUNERAL INFLUENCES

Portuguese Funerals

Death is a very solemn thing to the Portuguese. There are still very often professional mourners hired, entitled *carpideiras*. In this culture it is not uncommon to see a grieving widow wear black for a year, or even for her whole life.

In Portugal, the hearse is more like a large van with glass in the back so that the casket may be seen, and processions with the dead may involve many people walking along or behind it. Other times, the casket is carried on a large bier. Many times the people do not embalm, so burial may take place immediately. It is interesting to note that people may be dressed more casually, because they may be coming in from the fields or their job in order to attend the funeral or the wake.

Polish Funeral Culture

Long wakes with lots of food were very common in many Polish neighborhoods, but as people are becoming second and third generation, this is less likely. Historically, the family would be near as one was dying, and upon the death, the women would wail, and the doors would be flung open so that the soul could freely depart the body.

The body would be kept for three days at home. At certain churches in areas like Chicago or Milwaukee, you will find the complete funeral Mass still being offered in Polish. A Polish priest told me that three traditions prevail. These include the *exporta*, when the priest goes to the home or funeral home and escorts the body back to the church before the funeral begins. The other two involve hymnody. At most Polish funerals you will hear the hymn "Serdeczna Matko," which is set to the tune *Boże coś Polskę*, or "God Save our King." There is a beautiful octavo of it published by GIA Music. "Witaj Królowo Nieba," a version of the "Salve Regina," is usually sung at the cemetery. In some places it is common to sing this as they process to the cemetery, but others use it as the casket is being lowered into the ground. As guests disperse, close kin may stay until the grave has been filled in.

An obituary may not only be published in the paper, but along the side of a house. Another tradition is that the baptismal candle is present at one's death, and is placed in the coffin as well. This is to facilitate the path of the soul to the afterlife. In some places, there is still a special burial gown called a *śmiertelnica*, but more frequently this has been replaced by modest suits (https://culture.pl/en/article/7-weird-polish-funeral-customs). A year of mourning used to be observed by wearing a large black armband, but it is not uncommon to wear a small ribbon. On the death anniversary, a Mass is usually celebrated.

Italian Culture

There used to be a profound difference in Italian funerals based upon the class system. A simple Italian peasant had a very simple funeral, while a *signori* would have a very elaborate funeral with bands and lavish coffins and feasts. Through the years, Italian funerals have become more commercialized through the use of morticians and the limitations of the church and church cemeteries. It is common to have "Ombra mai fu" (from Handel's *Xerxes*) sung as a thanksgiving, or played instrumentally.

Italian floral arrangements had very specific designs and were thought to ward off evil spirits. Many of those designs remain and are still more elaborate today, but like many traditions, second and third generation immigrants often no longer understand their significance and symbolism.

Italians are likely to have three to four days of viewing before the funeral, and these are generally solemn affairs. Most funerals are open casket, and it is not uncommon to kiss the cheek of the deceased. Black is worn at the funeral, and for a period up to a year, though this may vary. Celebrating the death anniversary is very important in an Italian home. Often, a holy card is printed to remember the dead. It may have Jesus or Mary on one side, and the life and death dates or a brief eulogy on the other side. Sometimes it features a picture of the deceased.

Irish Wakes

Perhaps one of the most common funeral stereotypes we have is of the traditional Irish wake. In earlier years, the deceased was washed and laid out on the table at home, and when all came to pay their respects, it became a pretty good party, with flowing alcohol and laughter and stories—which turned to tears as the alcohol flowed even more! In this culture there were professional mourners known as "keeners." Surely there was drinking, but the mourning was and is an important part of the wake and more formal vigil. Placing the rosary within the fingers was very popular.

There is certainly no shortage of music that could be used both instrumentally and sung at Irish Catholic Funerals. Traditional songs like "Carrickfergus" and "I'll Take You Home Again, Kathleen" may find a place in the prelude. As I stated elsewhere in this book "O Danny Boy" is not liturgically appropriate for a funeral, but there are settings of the Song of Farewell to "Londonderry Air," and you can appease folks that way. Other popular selections may include "Morning Has Broken" or a version of the "Breastplate of Saint Patrick." Two newer hymns include "Christ in Me Arise" by Trevor Thompson and "The Cloud's Veil" by Liam Lawton. "Our Lady of Knock" is often sung as a thanksgiving piece.

The celebration continues after the funeral with a reception, and stopping by the house for a bite to eat. In more urban areas, these are now celebrated at a parish hall or private club.

ASIAN AND PACIFIC RIM CULTURES

Hmong Traditions

Many Hmong were original from China, before moving to Vietnam, Laos, or Thailand. Of the 100,000–140,000 Hmong in the United States, approximately ten percent are Catholics (https://www.cathedralsaintpaul.org/hmong-customs). The religious traditions of the Hmong are rooted in animism, meaning that when something good or evil happens to a person, a spirit has left them. The role of the village shaman to help restore balance is very important to them.

Death is really something felt by the entire community. Many from the village will present the family with money, and people travel from very far distances to attend family funerals or pay respects to someone from the same Laotian village.

Some of their funeral customs may seem strange to us, but they do not bury loved ones with buttons, zippers or metal closures; they have them removed from the coffin so that the deceased will not be hurt by hard objects.

The deceased may wear traditional or Western style dress, and it is not uncommon to place items in the casket. Historically, the Hmong drum and flute (*geej*) are often played, and the music is important to providing safe passage to the afterlife; though Catholic music may be more contemporary. One is not to show distress at a Hmong funeral. Even Catholic Hmong struggle with belief in the resurrection vs. reincarnation, but in any sense, there is a strong belief in the afterlife.

The Hmong community will still engage in a long wake period either in the home or at a communal center. The Catholic service takes on the traditional Hmong timeline, though the events are Christian. It will also include a ceremony called *Xem Tshwj*, which is a thank you during a spiritual release ritual. One ritual I looked at had a three day schedule which included:

Friday

10:00 AM	Gathering in presence of Body
12:00 PM	Lunch
2:00 PM	Funeral Rites
6:00 PM	Evening Prayer
7:30 PM	Dinner

Saturday

10:00 AM	Morning Prayer
12:00 PM	Lunch
5:00 PM	Evening Prayer
6:00 PM	Dinner
7:30 PM	Rosary
8:30 PM	Eulogy and Family Time

Sunday

10:00 AM	Morning Prayer
12:00 PM	Lunch
2:00 PM	Xem Tshwj
6:00 PM	Evening Prayer
8:00 PM	Txheeb Tswv Tooj lub neej

It is not uncommon to have a bilingual funeral, so that both the young and the old in the community may be involved, and the orders of worship are frequently printed in both languages. While there are many Hmong hymn texts, they are often set to traditional hymns. For example "LubNeej Tshiab Nyuob Saum Ntuj" is set to "Wayfaring Stranger" or "Ntuj Lub Txiaj Ntsim" is set to New Britain-Amazing Grace. Composers like Ricky Manolo are writing new hymns specifically for these cultures, and in recent years mainstream Catholic publishers have made materials much more accessible.

Philippine Funerals

In the Philippine culture, food is again a very prevalent element. Often wakes called *lamay* or *paglalamay* happen at the home of the deceased, rather than a funeral home and may last up to a week, and food is always present. The family will wear black or, if they wear white, a small black ribbon goes above the left breast.

After the funeral they offer a novena for the deceased, called a *pasiyam*, and celebrate the fortieth day after death with a Mass. This forty-day celebration is symbolic of Christ's forty days in the desert and the forty days from Easter to the Ascension. The first anniversary Mass is also an important celebration.

Funerals in China

In many Asian funerals, one sees yellow or white chrysanthemums as a symbol of lamentation and grief, and families will wear white mourning garments. Sometimes they are made of burlap. The casket is often white. Red is not worn, as it is the color of happiness. In China there are shrill-sounding instruments called *suona*, and there are professional mourners. In more rural areas, there may be no priest, so the ceremonies are family driven. What is very important to know about Catholic Asian culture is that it very different from other Asian funerals because it does not believe in ancestor worship, the use of spirit tablets, or burning money for the deceased. Catholic funerals and wakes do not burn incense sticks. Some elements, like giving the family money in a white envelope, may continue. Chinese Catholics are much less likely to cremate, but to bury the body whole, yet in recent years with the population surge, many city dwellers are cremated and rural folks are still simply buried.

Ironically, even if one is only nominally Catholic in China, they will give their parents a Catholic funeral rather than the Communist, secular alternative. Some Asians engage in ritual grave sweeping, but others only celebrate All Saints Day. In some regions the cultures still meld together and find their ways.

FUNERALS IN RELIGIOUS HOUSES

Perhaps the times when I've seen the *Order of Christian Funerals* lived out in its most complete form were the years that I was a member of a Benedictine Monastery. No matter what Order, the funeral is coupled with the charisms of that particular religious community. In his Rule, Saint Benedict reminded the monks to "Keep death daily before one's eyes" (Rule of Benedict 4:47), and we lived that. When a Sister was failing, it was often the younger nuns who were assigned to stay up at nights with her. Whether it was their gift or avocation, one learned to care for the ill and to be part of the process with them. As a young Sister, I was scared on my first night alone with a dying Sister. I recall trying to pray the Rosary or some prayer and got it all messed up. The Sister looked at me kindly and said, "Why don't you just go on to something you know?" This is where I learned that one of the best ways for me to pray with someone dying is to sing. It calmed the rasping breathing and let them sleep. It was here in the monastery that I learned not to fear death and to appreciate it.

After a Sister passed away, the funeral home was called to get the body. When they were ready, one of the Sisters would go into town to help dress the body. In one sense this was a modesty factor, but in the case of those who wore a full habit, it was to make sure all the garb got on right. Even when people went to simple veils or no habits, the tradition of a Sister helping to dress the body continued.

When Sister was ready to come home, the entire community lined the path that led from the front door to the chapel. The prioress would receive the body, in a manner similar to the Rite of Reception (OCF 37). As we brought the casket into the chapel of the dead, where she would remain until the funeral, we sang Lucien Deiss's "My Soul Is Longing for Your Peace."

That evening the Office of the Dead was prayed. She might remain in state just that evening, or for a full day. In front of the coffin was a prie-dieu and holy water, so that members and guests could pray for Sister.

At Vespers, the prioress or another individual would give a reflection on the life of the deceased, and there would be coffee and desserts afterward. These events were always very personalized. One Sister was from Pennsylvania, and had a huge sweet tooth. She always had candy on hand to give "the Fathers" and other men. (If you were a woman, tough luck!) So at the end of her vigil we passed out Hershey's chocolate bars.

The Mass of Christian Burial followed the ritual with no adaptations, other than that it was likely the superior of the community who would do the bulk of the preaching. The priests were monks from the neighboring abbey.

Strong smells of incense wafted as *In Paradisum* was sung in Latin as we left the church. Sisters were pallbearers, and the casket was placed in the hearse for the very short procession to the cemetery that was on our grounds. Everyone else walked in procession, singing simple Taizé ostinato chants along the way.

At the cemetery, the prioress led the Rite of Committal, and though guests may have departed back to the monastery and luncheon, the Sisters would continue standing and singing while the coffin was lowered into the ground, and while the green AstroTurf was pulled away, and the dark brown earth remained. Many would again sprinkle the casket and vault with holy water. There was something very fulfilling in the deeply tender process from the moment of welcoming the body home, to the vigil and funeral, and to seeing it through to the end. The starkness of the earth made it very real. It was keeping what Benedict said. Death was indeed before our eyes.

RURAL FUNERALS VS. METROPOLITAN FUNERALS

One of the most interesting things I have observed about funerals is the difference between funerals in small and large towns. I have no formal statistics but simply my own experience of living in different regions throughout the country. The parish I currently minister in is in a Milwaukee suburb of 30,000 people. As a parish, we have about 1600 families and 5300 members. In our church, which seats nearly 900, most funerals will only use the two main sections; and some very small funerals will just have immediate family of twenty or so people. While there are some daytime funerals, I would say most of ours are in the evening, with visitation taking place in the church narthex before, with no formal Vigil prayer. The evening service allows those who work to still attend. If it is an evening funeral, the burial will be the next day, and most people come to the luncheon afterward. For daytime funerals, after the funeral guests are invited to go to the cemetery for the Rite of Committal, and then they frequently return to the parish for a luncheon. Some don't go to the cemetery but wait with a cup of coffee for others to return. In this process, I would say about fifty percent of the guests stay for the luncheon, and the rest depart.

Last year, I went to a funeral located in a church in Milwaukee. We drove across town in procession over thirty minutes to get to the place of burial, and then it was probably another twenty-five minutes to the cultural center where the reception and meal were being held. So, from visitation to Mass to burial to reception, I went from 10:00 AM until 3:30 PM, a five-and-a-half-hour time commitment. I knew about five people there. I was very glad to be there, but when one looks at something like this, they can see how folks might just "slip in and slip out" for the visitation, or just attend the funeral.

Contrast this to my hometown in rural Montana. In a town of fifteen hundred people, everyone knows everyone. So there will be a full visitation in the afternoon and evening, followed by a Rosary or Vigil. Hundreds will come to pay their respects. The next day, the funeral will be plumb full, and many will process the mile to the cemetery and return to the parish hall. It may take as much time as the Milwaukee service described, but you are talking and connecting with the entire community. In the event of those really tragic funerals, then the funeral may end up in the high school gym or auditorium in order to accommodate the larger crowd. Because it is a rural region, it is not uncommon to see someone in their dress jeans, or wearing a clean pair of overalls. The standard of what is acceptable simply varies from region to region.

CHAPTER NINE

Remembering the Dead

THROUGHOUT THIS BOOK WE HAVE MADE A FEW BRIEF MENTIONS ABOUT HOW DIFFERENT CULTURES REMEMBER THE DEAD, BUT IT IS IMPORTANT TO TAKE A BROADER LOOK AT THE PICTURE. While some cultures may offer novenas, praying for the deceased for nine days, or other cultures celebrate a month, and others may celebrate a year, what is universal is All Saints Day and All Souls Day.

The list of the deceased members of the parish should be displayed in a book of the dead or in some other fashion throughout the month of November. In some parishes, the art and environment groups have created a fancy list, and in others it is contained within a simple book. Still other parishes invite loved ones to bring pictures of the deceased to be included in a display, with vigil candles, to remain there throughout the month.

In my parish, on November 2, we invite all those who have lost someone in the last year to come to a special All Souls Mass of remembrance that is open to the public. During the prayers of the faithful, we call out the name of each deceased member. Families may come up and take a candle and light it for their loved one and place it around our baptismal font, where it will remain throughout the week. As each name is called, a low-pitched bell is also rung.

In our sister parish across town, they invite people from any years to submit a photo of their loved one in advance, and there is a PowerPoint presentation as the names of the deceased are called out. One must be very careful in this type of situation, though. If the wrong name is called out with a picture, it could be very upsetting to the family members.

Throughout the year, families may have Masses said for their loved ones. There is usually a stipend to the parish for this. The names are always included in our prayers of the faithful and read aloud. Be sure and provide a phonetic spelling of any difficult names so as to avoid the hardship and disappointment of hearing the name of a loved one mispronounced.

Depending on the size of your parish, and the number of Mass intentions you receive, you may need to set a limit on how many Masses you offer for one person during a year. If so, perhaps you can help families find a religious order or a mission to take the additional Masses.

CONCLUSION

MUCH OF MY PASSION FOR WORKING WITH FUNERALS HAS COME OUT OF A SENSE THAT PEOPLE WERE LOSING TOUCH WITH WHAT A CATHOLIC, CHRISTIAN FUNERAL MEANS, and how important it is to minister well to them. As I am completing this project, I find myself ending up with the same premise I started with. It has been reaffirmed to me as I have read articles and books written by morticians, essayists, sociologists and psychologists, and theologians, and thought about what I have observed in our contemporary culture. Namely, we simply do not do death well any more. There are many reasons involved, including the increased secularization of our society, increased cremation, the continued sanitization of the funeral process, our distance from traditional customs, and the sheer size of our cities.

What has become increasingly obvious is that not only do we need to minister to people preparing for death or at the time of funerals, but we must find a way to explain what the Church stands for. There is an urgency here. We must stand up against the madness of the culture. This message must be preached from the pulpit and offered in presentations and in podcasts, bulletins, newsletters, children's religious ed programs, and any way we can.

We must be pastoral at the time of funerals, but "pastoral" is not synonymous with "doormat." It is our job to educate, and to be the keepers of the rite. If we cannot reverse these current trends, then it is our solemn task to do our best to keep them from getting worse. We must help those who come to us for funerals by preparing rich, vibrant liturgies that proclaim our faith and hope in the resurrection and that remind those present to pray for the dead, to pray not just at the funeral but every day. We may not want cookie-cutter funerals, but it is our task to make sure that they follow the wisdom and the structure given to us in the Rites themselves. Then will we know we have done a good job. Then we may rest in peace.

APPENDIX I

Brief Outline of Service

Prelude

Remarks of Remembrance

(optional—one person under five minutes)

Entrance Antiphon

Introductory Rites—Rite of Reception

Greeting

Blessing with Holy Water

Placing of Funeral Pall

Placing of Christian Symbols *(optional)*

Liturgy of the Word

First Reading from the Old Testament

Responsorial Psalm *(sung)*

Second Reading from the New Testament

Gospel *(read by priest or deacon)*

Homily

Prayers of the Faithful

Liturgy of the Eucharist

Offertory Procession and Hymn

Holy, Holy

Mystery of Faith

Amen

The Lord's Prayer

Sign of Peace

Lamb of God

Communion—*Catholics in good standing may receive communion. Others may come forward with arms folded for a blessing, or choose to remain in their pews*

Final Commendation

Invitation to Prayer

Silence

Signs of Farewell

Song of Farewell

Prayer of Commendation

Procession to the Place of Committal

In Paradisum (May the Angels)

APPENDIX II

Sheet for Service Preplanning or Parish Funeral Planning

You may wish to provide copies for safe deposit box, relatives, parish, and one to funeral home.

Name ______________________________

Date of Birth ______________________________

Date of Death ______________________________

Date and Time Vigil Service ______________________________

Date and Time Funeral Liturgy ______________________________

Burial/Commendation ______________________________

Luncheon in church hall? ______________________________

Celebrant ______________________________

Musician ______________________________

Server ______________________________

Funeral choir and cantor or solo cantor ______________________________

Funeral Service

Prelude ____

Remarks of Remembrance *(optional)*: One person may offer brief remarks before the funeral starts *(one page typed, 3-5 minutes)*

____

Entrance Antiphon

Placing the Funeral Pall on top of the casket ___________________

**Opening Song ____

Placing of Christian Symbols *(optional)*—Cross, Bible, Book of Gospels

First Reading (Old Testament) ___________________________

Read by ____

**Responsorial Psalm ___________________________________

Second Reading (New Testament) _________________________

Read by ____

Gospel ____________________

Proclaimed by priest or deacon.

Prayers of the Faithful *(text provided)*

____

Read by deacon if present or by family, friend, priest.

**Presentation of Gifts *(may be congregational, choir, or instrumental)*

____

Usually two to four people present the gifts.
Bread and wine are the only elements involved.

____

____

____

Communion: ☐ Body of Christ only ☐ Body and Blood of Christ

Typically three trained Extraordinary Ministers of Communion are needed. *(Note: This may vary depending on your church.)*

____

____

____

**Communion Song

____

**Thanksgiving Music *(optional)*

____

Song of Farewell Standard
Song of the Angels (*In Paradisum*) while casket is leaving church

**Additional Closing Song *(optional)*

____

Other special information

____

____

____

____

____

____

APPENDIX III

Scripture Readings and Key Phrases

Old Testament Scripture Readings

This is a summary of the Old Testament passages. Then the actual readings follow for you to see. Other Scriptures may be selected.

Job 19:1, 23-27	I know that my Redeemer lives. (p. ______)
Wisdom 3:1-9 *or* 3:1-6, 9	The souls of the just are in the hands of God. (p. ______)
Wisdom 4:7-15	The just man, though he die early, shall be at rest. (p. ______)
Isaiah 25:6, 7-9	On this mountain God will destroy death forever. God will save. (p. ______) *(Note: The reading calls for "6a" but include all of verse 6 for a more complete vision of the "heavenly banquet.")*
Lamentations 3:17-26	It is good to hope in silence for the saving help of the Lord. (p. ______)

DANIEL 12:1–3	Many of those who sleep in the dust of the earth shall awake. Those who lead the many to justice shall be like stars forever. (p. ______)
2 MACCABEES 12:43–46	It is good and holy to think of the dead rising again. (p. ______)

Additional selections not included in the Lectionary (8–22).

PROVERBS 31:10–31	A worthy wife/the valiant woman. (p. ______)
ECCLESIASTES 3:1–11	For everything there is a season. (p. ______)
SONG OF SONGS 2:8–14	Arise, my beloved, and come. (p. ______)
SONG OF SONGS 8:6–7	For stern as death is love, relentless is devotion. (p. ______)
SIRACH 44:1, 10–15	Praise for Godly men. (p. ______)
ISAIAH 35:1–6, 10	Those the Lord ransomed will return and enter Zion singing, crowned with everlasting joy. (p. ______)
ISAIAH 41:8–10, 13	"Fear not, I am with you." (p. ______)
ISAIAH 42:19	Earlier things have come to pass, new ones I foretell. (p. ______)
ISAIAH 57:15–19	I will give full comfort to them and to those who mourn them. (p. ______)

Isaiah 61:1-3	The spirit has called me to give them oil of gladness in place of mourning. (p. ______)
Isaiah 65:17-21	I create a Jerusalem to be a joy, full lives, no weeping, infants living life. (p. ______)
Ezekiel 34:11-16	Shepherd will tend flock, rescuing them from where they are scattered. (p. ______)
Ezekiel 37:12-14	You shall know I am the Lord, when I open your graves and you rise from them. (p. ______)
Micah 6:6-8	Do right, love goodness, and walk humbly with your God. (p. ______)
Zephaniah 3:16-20	I will bring you home and will gather you. (p. ______)

During Easter season you may substitute (found within the New Testament):

Acts 10:34-43 *or* 10:34-46, 42-43	God has appointed Jesus to judge every person, alive and dead. (p. ______)
Revelation 14:13	Blessed are the dead who die in the Lord finding rest from labors. (p. ______)
Revelation 20:11—21:1	The book of life is opened, and the dead were judged by their deeds. Visions of new heaven. (p. ______)

REVELATION 21:1–5A, 6B–7	God will wipe every tear from their eyes. There will be no more death or mourning. (p. ______)

New Testament Scripture Readings

This is a summary of the New Testament passages. Then the actual readings follow for you to see. Other Scriptures may be selected.

ACTS 10:34–43 *OR* 10:34–46, 42–43	God has appointed Jesus to judge every one, alive and dead. (p. ______)
ROMANS 5: 5–11	Hope does not disappoint, for God's love has been poured on us. Reconciled to God, we will be saved through Jesus' death. (p. ______)
ROMANS 5:17–21	How much more will those who receive the abundance of grace and of the gift of justification come to reign in life through the one person Jesus Christ. (p. ______)
ROMANS 6:3–9 *OR* 6:3–4, 8–9	We were baptized into death, so that we shall also live with Christ. Let us walk in newness of life. (p. ______)
ROMANS 8:14–23	We groan within ourselves as we wait for the redemption of our bodies. (p. ______)
ROMANS 8:31B–35, 37–39	What will separate us from the love of Christ? Nothing can take us from the love of God in Christ Jesus our Lord. (p. ______)

Romans 14:7-9, 10b-12	Whether alive or dead, we belong to the Lord. (p. ______)
1 Corinthians 15:20-23, 24b-28 *or* 15:20-23	All people will be brought to life in Christ. The last enemy to be destroyed is death (p. ______)
1 Corinthians 15:51-57	Death is swallowed up in victory. (p. ______)
2 Corinthians 4:14—5:1	For we know if our earthly dwelling is destroyed we have a building from God, a dwelling not made with hands, eternal in heaven. (p. ______)
2 Corinthians 5:1, 6-10	We have an everlasting home in heaven. (p. ______)
Philippians 3:20-21	Citizens in heaven, Jesus will transfigure our bodies to his glorious body. (p. ______)
Thessalonians 4:13-18	Do not grieve those fallen asleep. We shall stay with the Lord forever. (p. ______)
2 Timothy 2:8-13	If we have died with him, we shall live with him. (p. ______)
1 John 3:1-2	We shall see God as he really is. (p. ______)
1 John 3:14-16	We have passed from death to life because we love our brothers and sisters. (p. ______)
Revelation 14:13	Blessed are the dead who die in the Lord... finding rest from labors. (p. ______)

REVELATION 20:11—21:1	The book of life is opened, and the dead were judged by their deeds. Vision of new heaven. (p. ______)
REVELATION 21:1-5A, 6B-7	God will wipe every tear from their eyes. There will be no more death or mourning. (p. ______)

Additional readings not included in the Lectionary.

1 CORINTHIANS 13:1-8	If I speak with human tongue but have not love. (p. ______)
EPHESIANS 3:14-21	Don't lose heart over afflictions. The love of Christ surpasses knowledge. (p. ______)
2 TIMOTHY 4:6-8, 17-18	I am being poured out like a libation. I competed well, finished the race, I kept faith. (p. ______)
1 PETER 1:3-9	Though you suffer through trials, this proves genuineness of faith, achieving your salvation. (p. ______)
REVELATION 22:1-7	They will look upon God's face, and his name will be on their foreheads. (p. ______)

Gospel Scripture Readings (to be proclaimed by deacon or priest)

This is a summary of the Gospel passages. Then the actual readings follow for you to see. ***Please note:*** *Many of the passages suggested deal with Jesus' death and resurrection, and may be difficult. Here the most popular and comfortable readings have been bolded.*

MATTHEW 5:1-12A	**Beatitudes—Rejoice and be glad, for your reward shall be great in heaven.** (p. ______)
MATTHEW 11:25-30	**Come to me and I will give you rest.** (p. ______)
MATTHEW 25:1-13	The bridegroom comes. Go out and meet him. (p. ______)
MATTHEW 25:31-46	**Whatsoever you do to the least of my people, that you do unto me. Come, you whom my Father has blessed.** (p. ______)
MARK 15:33—16:6	Jesus gave a loud cry and breathed his last. (p. ______)
LUKE 7:11-17	Jesus said, "Young man, I say to you, arise." (p. ______)
LUKE 12:35-40	Be prepared, for at an hour you do not expect. (p. ______)
LUKE 23:33-43	Today you will be with me in paradise. (p. ______)
LUKE 23:44—24:6A	Father, I put my life in your hands. (p. ______)

LUKE 24:13-35	Was it not necessary that the Christ should suffer. (p. ______)
JOHN 5:24-29	**All who believe in the Son will have eternal life.** (p. ______)
JOHN 6:37-40	**All who believe in the Son will have eternal life and I will raise them to life again on the last day.** (p. ______)
JOHN 6:51-58	**All who eat this bread will live forever and I will raise them up on the last day.** (p. ______)
JOHN 11:17-27 *OR* 11:21-27	I am the resurrection and the life. Whoever believes in me even if he dies will live, and everyone who lives and believes in me will never die. (p. ______)
JOHN 11:32-45	Jesus consoles Mary and Martha on the death of Lazarus, and calls him to wake from the dead, "Lazarus, come out." (p. ______)
JOHN 12:23-28 *OR* 12:23-26	If a grain of wheat falls on the ground and dies, it yields a rich harvest. (p. ______)
JOHN 14:1-6	**There are many rooms in my Father's house.** (p. ______)
JOHN 17:24-26	Father, the world does not know you, but I know you, and they know that you sent me. (p. ______)
JOHN 19:17-18, 25-30	Jesus bowed his head and gave up his spirit. (p. ______)

Additional readings not found in Lectionary.

MATTHEW 6:19-23	Why are you anxious? Learn how the wildflowers grow....Seek first the kingdom of God. (p. ______)
LUKE 1:67-74	Jesus came to bring salvation, to shine on those who sit in darkness and death's shadow. (p. ______)
JOHN 3:13-17	The Son of Man must be lifted up so everyone who believes in him may have eternal life. (p. ______)
JOHN 10:11-18, 27-30	My sheep hear my voice. I give them eternal life and they shall never perish. (p. ______)

Funerals of Baptized Children

ISAIAH 25:6, 7-9	On this mountain God will destroy death forever. God will save. (p. ______) *(Note: The reading calls for "6a" but include all of verse 6 for a more complete vision of the "heavenly banquet.")*
LAMENTATIONS 3:22-26	It is good to hope in silence for the saving help of the Lord. (p. ______)
ROMANS 6:3-4, 8-9	We were baptized into death, so that we shall also live with Christ. Let us walk in newness of life. (p. ______)

ROMANS 14:7-9	Whether alive or dead, we belong to the Lord. (p. ______)
1 CORINTHIANS 15:20-23	All people will be brought to life in Christ. (p. ______)
REVELATION 21:1A, 3-5	There will be no more death or mourning. (p. ______)
MATTHEW 11:25-30	You have hidden these things from the learned and the clever and revealed them to children. (p. ______)
MARK 10:13-16	The kingdom of heaven belongs to little children. (p. ______)
JOHN 6:37-40 *OR* 6:37-39	This is the will of my Father, that I should lose nothing of all that he has given to me. (p. ______)
JOHN 6:51-58	All who eat this bread will live for ever, and I will raise them up on the last day. (p. ______)
JOHN 11:32-38, 40	If you believe, you will see the glory of God. (p. ______)
JOHN 19:25-30	This is your mother. (p. ______)

Readings not included in the lectionary that sometimes are appropriate.

ISAIAH 49:1, 14–16	Can a mother forget her infant? I will not forget. (p. ______)
JEREMIAH 31:15–17	Rachel weeps for her children....There is hope for your future. (p. ______)

Funerals for Children Who Died Before Baptism

ISAIAH 25:6A, 7–8B	The Lord will destroy death for ever. (p. ______)
LAMENTATIONS 3:22–26	It is good to wait in silence for the Lord God to save. (p. ______)
MATTHEW 11:25–30	You have hidden these things from the learned and the clever and have revealed them to children. (p. ______)

APPENDIX IV

Summary Sheet for Parish Website or as a Handout

This may vary greatly depending on the formality of your parish. This is a modification of several parish sheets combined to provide an example.

This Church provides:

- Use of the parish hall for a reception
- Parish funeral staff
- A funeral planner
- Members of the bereavement team
- Musicians for the liturgy
- An order of worship for the funeral

Funeral Participants:

- Family will be in first pews.
- Guest priests and deacons are welcome as long as arrangements have been made in advance and they have their faculties.
- Pallbearers are seated in a section.

- Lectors may be families and friends.
- Gift bearers may be family and friends.
- Extraordinary Ministers of Communion must be practicing Catholics who are already trained in advance.
- Musicians—Only parish musicians are used, as they are familiar with the liturgical rites, the equipment, and the acoustics of this space.
- The resurrection choir is available.
- Additional instrumentalists may be made available upon request and for additional fees.

LITURGICAL FURNISHINGS:

- The liturgical environment reflects the appropriate liturgical season and may not be moved.
- Please refrain from artificial flowers.
- You may place one flower arrangement in front of the ambo, and another in front of the altar.
- All arrangements must be removed after the liturgy/ or flowers may remain in the church.

FUNERAL TIMETABLE:

Morning Funeral

11:00 AM visitation
12:00 PM beginning of funeral
1:00 PM end of funeral
1:00 PM beginning of lunch
2:30 PM departure for cemetery

Afternoon Funeral

12:00 PM	visitation
1:00 PM	beginning of funeral
2:00 PM	end of funeral
2:30 PM	beginning of lunch
4:00 PM	departure for cemetery

FEE STRUCTURE:

Use of the church *(includes printing of the orders of worship, lights, and heat/air)*	________
Use of church hall *(not including catering)*	________
Priest/deacon	________
Altar server	________
Keyboard player	________
Cantor	________
Other musicians	________

APPENDIX V

Parish Flow Chart for Funerals

Who takes the initial calls for funeral? Priest? Liturgist? Administrative Assistant? Pastoral Associate?

Who reserves space for the funeral and calendars the event?

What rooms will be needed? Narthex? family room? church? parish hall? Multipurpose room?

Will there be a special setup needed in hall? Who does?

Is there a priest or deacon assigned for the funeral?

Is there a minister scheduled for the funeral vigil and committal?

Who is meeting with the family to plan the funeral?

Who will contact musician, cantor, and resurrection choir?

Who will contact servers?

Are parish ministers needed for ushers, lectors, and communion? Who will contact?

Who records the deceased for the prayers of the faithful?

Who records the deceased for the bulletin?

Who records the deceased in the parish records?

Which funeral home is being used?

Who is the family contact for the funeral?

Will there be a Luncheon? Number? Who is preparing/catering?

Who creates and prints orders of worship?

Who meets the family on day of funeral?

Who walks through ministries with family members?

Who will turn on heat/air, sound system, lights?
How far in advance?

Are there special audiovisual needs? Showing a presentation?
Recording liturgy?

Are there any unique circumstances?

Are additional parish staff or volunteers needed?

APPENDIX VI

Frequently Asked Questions about Death and Funerals

Is "The Anointing of the Sick" the same as "Last Rites"? What about "Viaticum"?

The sick may be anointed any time it is a serious illness. When we think of the dying, and speak of the Last Rites, only a priest or bishop can administer the sacraments of penance and anointing of the sick. In the absence of a priest these sacraments cannot be administered, but a lay person may give a dying person Holy Communion, which in this case is "Viaticum, the last sacrament of the Christian."

What is the Catholic Teaching on Purgatory and Limbo?

The *Catechism of the Catholic Church* defines purgatory as a "purification, so as to achieve the holiness necessary to enter the joy of heaven," which is experienced by those "who die in God's grace and friendship, but still imperfectly purified" (CCC 1030). It notes that "this final purification of the elect...is entirely different from the punishment of the damned" (CCC 1031). This purification is necessary because we may die with mortal sins forgiven, but we still may be impure or may have many sins. This is why we pray for the deceased at the Mass of the Christian Burial, and why people offer Masses for the deceased.

In 2007, the church reversed her position on limbo in a forty-one-page document, stating "The conclusion of this study is that there are theological and liturgical reasons to hope that infants who die without baptism may be saved and brought into eternal happiness even if there is not an explicit teaching on this question found in revelation." Happily it also said, "There are reasons to hope that God will save these infants precisely because it was not possible (to baptize them)." http://www.vatican.va/roman_curia/congregations/cfaith/cti_documents/rc_con_cfaith_doc_20070419_un-baptised-infants_en.html

What are the three parts of the Catholic Funeral?

There are three main parts: 1) the Vigil, 2) the Funeral Liturgy (with or without Mass), and 3) the Rite of Committal. Besides these, other rites are provided, e.g., prayers just after death, prayers for gathering in the presence of the body at the beginning of a visitation, and prayers for transferring the body to the church.

How does a homily differ from a eulogy?

A homily breaks open the Scripture readings that have been proclaimed, while a eulogy ("to speak well of someone") praises the deceased. The homily takes its theme from the biblical readings and speaks in general of the Catholic belief in the resurrection, life after death, and the qualities of Christian living. The virtues of the deceased can be cited as examples. A homily is appropriate at the Vigil or the Funeral Mass. A eulogy is more appropriate when spoken at the funeral home during the visitation, the Vigil, or at a family gathering after the Rite of Committal.

What is appropriate to use in a family's "remarks of remembrance"?

"Remarks of remembrance" occur right before the funeral begins. The family is seated, and the priest invites the speaker forward. Only one relative or friend should speak. These remarks are not to be a eulogy but, rather, a brief word of thanksgiving for the life of the deceased. These remarks are optional. If done, the remarks should be concise and written out beforehand. They should be three to five minutes long.

How does the Church handle cremation?

(*Note:* This is a brief summary of cremation. There is more detailed information on pages 31-36.)

- Cremation is allowed, but the church prefers the body to be at the funeral and for cremation to take place later if at all possible.
- If someone is cremated, there must be a worthy sealed container (urn) for the remains.
- [In my parish] At the time of the funeral itself, the urn will be placed in the large ossuary by the staff of the funeral home and placed in the sanctuary. In the tradition of this parish, the family does not carry the ossuary during the processions. It will be removed after the liturgy.
- Ashes may not be spread, divided among relatives, or made into jewelry.
- Ashes are to be buried.

Must we use a funeral home?

It is preferred that you use a funeral home. The parish is not equipped with guest books, easels, or to help move the guests, and manage timing of a visitation.

Can we use pre-recorded music?

You may play music during the visitation, but there is no recorded music and no secular music allowed during the liturgy itself.

GLOSSARY

anointing of the sick - When a priest visits the sick and anoints them with a holy oil. This sacrament may be repeated on numerous occasions during one's lifetime and is a sacrament for the living. It is frequently combined with confession and communion. Sometimes it is mistakenly called "the Last Rites."

casket - A container designated for human remains for a funeral. It is usual constructed of wood or metal, and is often lined with fabric.

Christian symbols - Cross, Bible, rosary that may be placed on top of the casket at the funeral service.

closed casket - When the casket is literally closed at the visitation.

columbarium - A room or a niche where funeral urns may be stored permanently. It could be freestanding, or part of a mausoleum. Many cemeteries have them, and some churches build a space for them.

cortege - The solemn procession as people walk behind the casket to the church or cemetery.

cremation - The act of reducing the body to ashes by fire. This usually takes place over several hours in a very hot incinerator.

cremated remains - A term for the ashes of one who has been cremated. This term is sometimes shortened into the term "Cremains" but that is not as dignified.

Committal (Rite of Committal) - The final portion of the funeral that takes place at the graveside or place of rest.

disposition - Placement of urn or coffin in final resting place.

embalming - Preserving the body for display by injecting it with special fluids.

Extreme Unction - Final communion may be distributed by a priest or a lay person.

Funeral Mass - Takes place at a church, following the *Order of Christian Funerals.*

funeral spray - Flowers specifically prepared to be draped on the casket.

holy water - This is water that has been blessed, and is a symbol of our baptism, and as a cleansing for our sins. It is used to bless the casket, urn, or ossuary. It is used when people make the sign of the cross to bless themselves.

interment - The actual act of burying a coffin. Takes place at the cemetery.

Last Rites - Before a person dies they may see the priest for anointing, reconciliation, and communion. It is a sacrament for the living.

Masses for the Dead - People may have Masses offered in honor of the dead. The purpose is to pray for their souls in purgatory.

memorial cards - Small printed cards which may include a holy picture, or a Scripture verse, and the name and dates of the deceased on the reverse. Usually these are purchased through the funeral home or a local printer.

memorial service - Service to remember the deceased where there is no body present. It does not have the funeral introductory rites or the final commendation.

Order of Worship - A booklet that is usually provided by the church to help one through the service. Sometimes called a worship aid or a program.

Order of Christian Funerals - The documents that guide us in celebrating all aspects of a Catholic funeral.

pall - the white cloth that is draped over the casket. It is a symbol of our baptismal promises and our hope in the resurrection.

Remarks of Remembrance - Allowing a family member to speak at the funeral about the deceased. This is not a eulogy.

urn - the container that is used for the sacred remains of someone who has been cremated. They are available in many different styles, and of varying materials, and prices, but they should bring dignity to the remains.

vigil - Service held on the eve before the funeral at the end of visitation. Typically involves Scriptures and prayers. A Rosary is sometimes involved. It may be known as a "wake."

visitation - A time when people may come and pay their respects to the family, and view the casket if there is one.

wake - The time of keeping vigil before a funeral. May be one evening or several days. It often ends with a prayer service with Scripture known as a Vigil, or with a Rosary.

BIBLIOGRAPHY

Champlin, Joseph. *Through Death to Life*. Ave Maria Press, 2002.

Gilmour, Peter and David A. Lysik. *Now and at the Hour of Our Death: Instructions Concerning My Death and Funeral*. Liturgy Training Publications, 1996.

Kalish, Richard A., ed. "Death and Dying: Views from Many Cultures" in *Omega-Journal of Death and Dying*. Baywood Publishing Company, Inc., 1972–1977.

Kohler, Kenneth. *Preparing a Catholic Funeral*. Living the Good News, 2003.

Marchal, Michael. *Parish Funerals*. Liturgy Training Publications, 1987.

McCarthy, Flor, S.D.B. *Funeral Liturgies*. First Dominican Publications, 1987.

Rutherford, Richard and Tony Barr. *The Death of a Christian: The Order of Christian Funerals*. The Liturgical Press, 1990.

Smith, Margaret. *Facing Death Together: Parish Funerals*. Liturgy Training Publications, 1989.

Taylor, Richard P. *Death and the Afterlife: A Cultural Encyclopedia*. ABC-CLIO, 2000.

Turner, Paul. *Light in the Darkness: Preparing Better Catholic Funerals*. The Liturgical Press, 2017.

http://factsanddetails.com/china/cat3/sub14/item101.html#chapter-1

https://en.wikipedia.org/wiki/Funeral_practices_and_burial_customs_in_the_Philippines

http://www.italianancestry.com/mathias/

http://www.indiana.edu/~famlygrf/culture/esirman.html

http://blog.adw.org/2018/01/gift-african-american-catholic-tradition/

https://abcnews.go.com/US/dead-people-life-poses-funerals/story?id=23456853

https://press.vatican.va/content/salastampa/en/bollettino/pubblico/2016/10/25/161025c.html

Telephone Interview – Betty Ann Hickey, Archdiocese of New Orleans, Associate Director of Worship Office: July 16, 2018

Information supplied by the Hmong Community of Sheboygan, Wisconsin

OF RELATED INTEREST

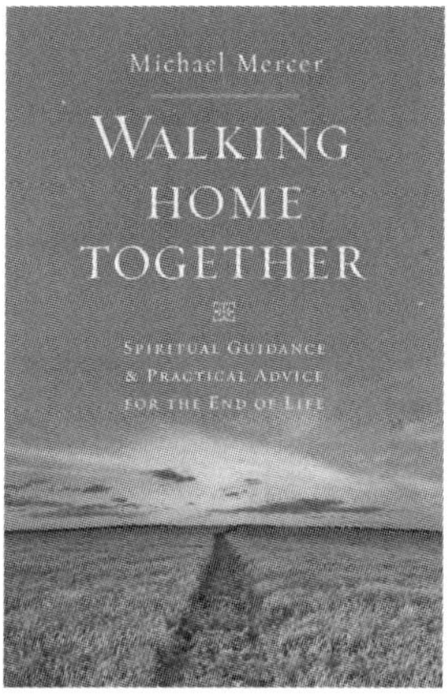

Walking Home Together

Spiritual Guidance & Practical Advice for the End of Life

CHAPLAIN MICHAEL MERCER

Very few books address this sensitive subject, and none do so more beautifully than Mike Mercer's tender and practical guide. In the tradition of Nouwen and Rolheiser, he offers thoughts, practices, stories, and prayers that can bring comfort and strength for those in their final season of life. *Where will I find love right now? How is my death a gift for others? How can I cope when I'm so afraid?* Mercer explores these difficult questions as well as practical considerations like advance directives as he helps readers immerse themselves in the powerful love of the Good Shepherd, who always walks this journey with us.

128 PAGES | $14.95 | 5½" x 8½" | ORDER 851497 | 9781627851497

Habits of Resilience

Learning to Live Fully in the Midst of Loss

A Grief Workbook

BERYL SCHEWE

Certified chaplain Beryl Schewe shares stories of people and communities—those who are dying and those who live on—and offers 13 practical habits of resilience to move us beyond grief and back to a full, rich life. This moving, hopeful workbook includes gentle reflection questions and a 21-day gratitude challenge. Written for those who grieve, as well as for caregivers and pastoral ministers, it is a sure companion for anyone who seeks healing, and for all who need to remember that love always triumphs over death.

144 PAGES | $16.95 | 6" x 9" | ORDER 851053 | 9781627851053